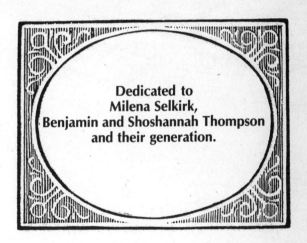

Dedicated to
Milena Selkirk,
Benjamin and Shoshannah Thompson
and their generation.

Table of Contents

Who was John F. Kennedy?

Was he a rich glamour boy whose father bought him the White House?

Was he a Cold Warrior ready to provoke a fight to prove his manliness?

Was he a political animal whose every move was calculated to win votes?

Or was he just another foggy liberal, who let his lofty ideals get in the way of governing?

John F. Kennedy was the 35th President of the United States. He was the youngest man ever elected to the White House. He was also the first Chief Executive to be born in the Twentieth Century. Few other leaders in history so embraced the necessity of change and progress.

"Those who make peaceful revolution impossible, make violent revolution inevitable."

—JFK

He called his Administration the NEW FRONTIER. It was supposed to involve more than the usual campaign slogans. "It is not a set of promises," Jack Kennedy declared. "It sums up not what I intend to offer the American people, but what I intend to ask of them."

The New Frontier challenged all citizens to make the sacrifices necessary to preserve freedom at home and abroad. It meant a healthy, modernized economy. A dedication to education and scientific research. A government that took the lead in protecting the poor and powerless. And a nation strong enough to make peace with its enemies.

Whatever his successes and failures, there can be no doubt that JFK changed the way Americans thought about themselves and their country. Suddenly no problem seemed too big to handle, even flying to the moon.

In the international sphere, Jack Kennedy's obvious charm and intelligence won friends for America all over the world. And at home, his personal courage and commitment inspired a generation of young people to get involved with the great issues of the day: freedom and equality, war and peace.

What then is the legacy of JFK? Is it nothing more than nostalgia for the Golden Age of Camelot, when everyone in Washington seemed more vigorous, charming, and attractive than today? Or was there something rare about this individual that was of his time—and yet for all times?

Who was this President who challenged an entire nation to live up to its own highest ideals?

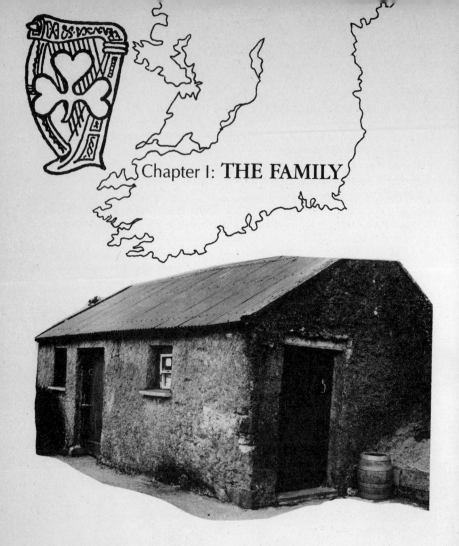

Chapter I: **THE FAMILY**

The first Kennedy in America left no photograph or documents behind him. We know that his name was Patrick Kennedy. That he was 26 years old in 1848, the year that he left the family farm in County Wexford, Ireland, and took a boat across the Atlantic. And that he was the last member of the family to die in poverty and obscurity.

We also know that Ireland was in the grip of a Great Famine. A fungus attacking the staple food of the island—potatoes—first made its appearance in 1845. The blight often spoiled a whole year's worth of food in a matter of days or hours, converting the precious tubers into a smelly black ooze, poisonous even to livestock.

Over the next ten years, a million men, women, and children would die of hunger. At least another million would leave the country forever. The absentee landlords, many of them rich Englishmen, did little to help the starving poor. Some got rid of useless mouths by paying their fares over to Australia or America. It mattered little. Ireland was just another backward colony of the great British Empire.

9

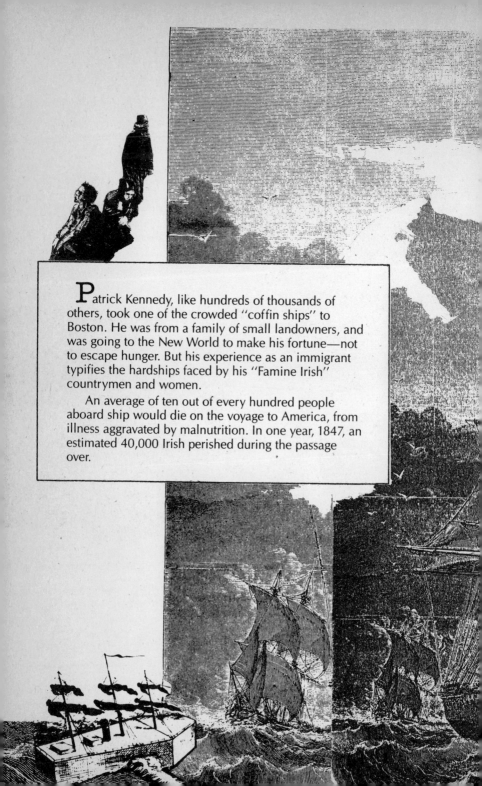

Patrick Kennedy, like hundreds of thousands of others, took one of the crowded "coffin ships" to Boston. He was from a family of small landowners, and was going to the New World to make his fortune—not to escape hunger. But his experience as an immigrant typifies the hardships faced by his "Famine Irish" countrymen and women.

An average of ten out of every hundred people aboard ship would die on the voyage to America, from illness aggravated by malnutrition. In one year, 1847, an estimated 40,000 Irish perished during the passage over.

Packed tightly together in the stinking steerage compartments below decks—this was probably as close as any Europeans would ever come to the horrors endured by Africans destined for the slave markets of the South.

Once in America things were not much better. By 1850, one-third of Boston was Irish and Roman Catholic. The immigrants were crowded into tiny apartments and dank cellars all over the city's "Paddyvilles" —urban Irish ghettos. They took whatever hard, dirty work they could find along the waterfront or in nearby factories. All learned quickly that the good citizens of Boston, mostly Protestants of English or Scottish descent, regarded them as something less than human.

Patrick Kennedy met his wife, Bridget Murphy, on the boat over. They married soon after their arrival in Boston. When he could find work, Patrick slaved away on the docks unloading ships. Eventually he found a better job as a cooper, making barrels. He spent the rest of life within the poverty of East Boston. Here the Irish were packed so tightly together that they managed to maintain a precarious degree of security.

The Kennedys had three daughters and a son, Patrick Joseph, born 1858. A year later, Patrick Kennedy, founder of the clan, died of cholera. Bridget was forced to take a job clerking in a notions shop. After years of saving, she was finally able to buy the shop and better the fortunes of her family.

All the women in family regarded young Patrick Joseph as the key to their salvation. They pampered him, and encouraged his ambition. As a teenager, P.J., as he came to be known, started work on the docks. Like his mother, he saved for years to be able to buy his own business: a rundown saloon near Haymarket Square.

It was in his new role as entrepreneur that P.J. learned how America really worked: money created a base for political power. Power, when properly managed, usually produced money. On and on. It was a lesson he would never forget.

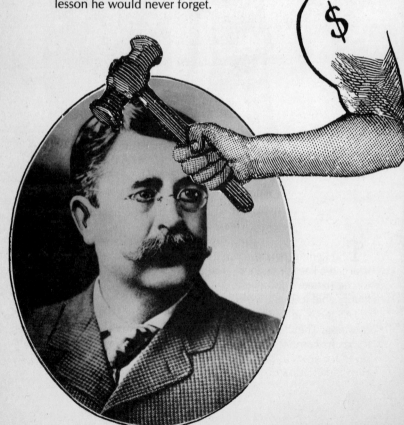

14

Boston at that time was dominated by an elite sometimes referred to as Brahmins—because of their "pure" bloodlines going back all the way to the Pilgrims. They were so snooty that it was said they only spoke to each other, and to God.

Protestant, prosperous, and exceedingly proper, the Brahmins struggled for decades to keep real power out of the hands of the Irish. First they tried to change the residency requirements for voting from 5 to 25 years. When that failed, they banded together to let the newcomers know that No Irish Need Apply for any decent job or housing.

15

Yet the Brahmin's plan to segregate the Irish backfired totally.
By concentrating them, it made the immigrants a tremendous
political force. By the 1870s, local Irish barroom and block
organizations took over the Democratic party. They created a
shadow government that delivered all the jobs, services, and
security they were denied by the Brahmins who ran the
Republican party—and the rest of Massachusetts.

Similar systems were also developing in New York, Chicago,
and other urban areas. District leaders, usually called "ward
bosses," ran the different neighborhoods. The boss often met
shiploads of immigrants right at the docks. The newcomers were
welcomed, and told what they could expect in return for votes and
loyalty: everything from a job and a turkey on Thanksgiving, to
help finding an apartment and a doctor that would care for the
kids on credit.

P.J. Kennedy was smart, energetic, and sober. Soon, he was able
to buy a second saloon, and branched out with investments in a
hotel and other businesses. In 1886—the year in which immigrant
children first outnumbered the children of Yankees in Boston—P.J.
parlayed his business success into political power. A cornerstone
of the community, he was elected to the State Senate.

A year later, he married Mary Augusta Hickey, the attractive daughter of an established Irish businessman. From that time on, it would become a Kennedy tradition to marry women of a higher social class.

In 1888, Boston elected its first Irish-American mayor. This signalled that the way was open for other careers in government, civil service, and naturally, the police. In the same year, Mary Augusta gave birth to her first child...

Joseph, who would later become the father of America's first Catholic President.

If it had been up to P.J., the boy would likely have been called Patrick. But the new mother insisted on a name that wouldn't sound so "Irish." Throughout her life, she encouraged Joseph to stress the upperclass "lace curtain" rather than the "shanty" Irish side of his background. And like most of the Kennedy wives to follow, she had little regard for the rough and tumble world of politics.

An Irish Jig.

17

One of P.J.'s bitterest rivals was a young upstart named John F. Fitzgerald. Later known as Honey Fitz for his honey-tongued oratory, Fitzgerald was fearless, defiant, and proud of his heritage. A natural politician, he seemed to know the faces, names, and life stories of everyone in his ward. Eventually he was elected Mayor of the city. Who could've imagined then that one day Honey Fitz would become related to the Kennedy clan through marriage?

Even when Fitzgerald was sent to Washington as a congressman, he refused to forget his roots. He led the opposition to a proposed new law barring any immigrant who couldn't read the U.S. Constitution. Boston Brahmin Senator Henry Cabot Lodge, was incensed:

LODGE
"You are an impudent young man. Do you think Jews or Italians have any right to this country?"

FITZGERALD
"As much as your father or mine. After all, it's only a difference of a few ships."

18

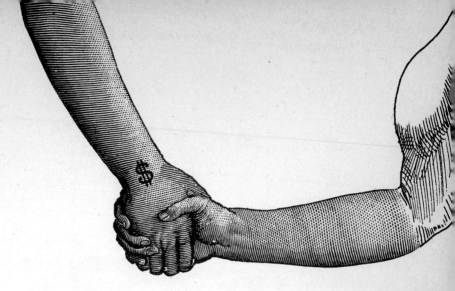

This was one of Fitzgerald's few *philosophical* conflicts. He was much more interested in practical politics. And like P.J. Kennedy, he quickly learned the link between money and power. Once in power, Honey Fitz proceeded to get reasonably rich by publishing a Boston newspaper. Local businessmen who wanted to win his favor advertised lavishly. The paper, in turn, was used to advance Fitzgerald's political ambitions and those of his friends.

Joseph Kennedy thrived in this world—though he was destined to outgrow it. The boy was even more ambitious than his father, and looked upon making money as a chance to demonstrate his ample abilities. Throughout his youth he held jobs of every kind. At age 12, he started work as a delivery boy for a posh Boston shop. His mother advised him not to seem too "Irish," too much of a "Kennedy".

The boy avidly read the rags-to-riches Horatio Alger novels, popular at the time. When it was time for college, he entered Harvard. Like all Catholics, he was something of a social "untouchable," and a target for religious slurs and slights. Yet he was determined to succeed. An unashamed social climber, Joe made friends with top football players and other campus celebrities. His goal was to make a million dollars by the time he was thirty-five.

While still in college, he started courting Rose Fitzgerald, the tall, attractive daughter of Honey Fitz. Her parents tried to discourage this relationship with the son of a saloon keeper and political rival. Yet the persistent Kennedy would not be frightened off.

Joe graduated Harvard in 1912 and immediately used his father's connections to land himself a choice job as State bank examiner. This helped him make his own contacts. At age 25, he took control of the Irish-owned Columbia Trust, and became the nation's youngest bank president.

Rose, meanwhile, attended an exclusive Catholic convent school which promised to teach her:

"...Tact, quiet courage, and the willingness to subordinate her will to another's gracefully and even gaily."

In her future life with Joseph Kennedy, Rose would need all of these qualities and more. The couple finally married in 1914. A year later, Rose had the first of her nine children:

Joseph, Jr. By temperament, appearance, and seniority within the tight family structure, the boy was clearly the Kennedy *crown prince* and chosen successor.

21

In 1917, another son was born. He was named John Fitzgerald, after Rose's father. Almost from the start, the boy was thin and sickly. At three years old, he almost died of scarlet fever. And for practically the rest of his life he suffered from diseases of the blood and other disabilities.

With America's entry in World War I, Joe Sr. became manager of a shipyard owned by Bethlehem Steel. He was paid the regal salary of $20,000 a year at a time when the average wage was probably $1,000 or less. Under Kennedy's energetic management, the shipyard easily exceeded production schedules. And the family also continued to grow.

In 1918, the Kennedy's had their third child, Rosemary. Not for several years would it become clear that the pretty little girl had been born retarded.

The following year saw the birth of Kathleen, a lively, rebellious girl, propelled into the first rank of the children by Rosemary's disability.

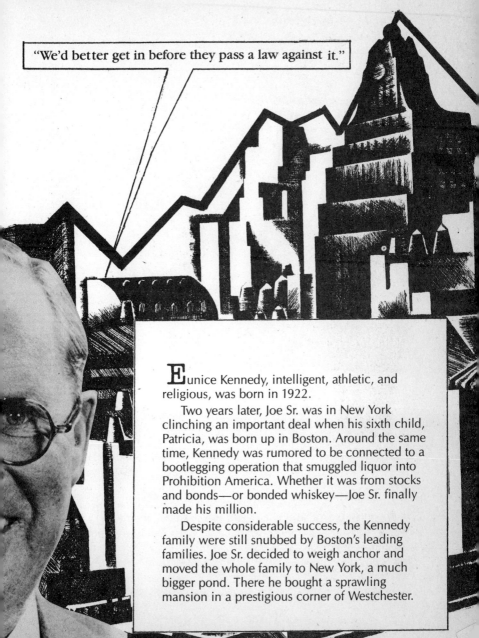

Right after the war, Joe Sr. decided to enter the stock business. It was just before the ten year boom that really made the Twenties roar. He gave up his shipyard job and took a hefty cut in pay. Kennedy knew that he could use inside information to invest without risk. He practically smelled a killing in speculation.

"We'd better get in before they pass a law against it."

Eunice Kennedy, intelligent, athletic, and religious, was born in 1922.

Two years later, Joe Sr. was in New York clinching an important deal when his sixth child, Patricia, was born up in Boston. Around the same time, Kennedy was rumored to be connected to a bootlegging operation that smuggled liquor into Prohibition America. Whether it was from stocks and bonds—or bonded whiskey—Joe Sr. finally made his million.

Despite considerable success, the Kennedy family were still snubbed by Boston's leading families. Joe Sr. decided to weigh anchor and moved the whole family to New York, a much bigger pond. There he bought a sprawling mansion in a prestigious corner of Westchester.

HOLLYW✡✡D

Through business contacts, Joe began to get involved with the growing movie industry. He had faith in mass communications and believed it would help educate the masses, as well as make fortunes for those smart enough to get in, in time.

Confidently, he vowed to take the business away from Jewish "pants pressers" like the Goldwyns and Warners, men who supposedly started out as tailors and somehow built an empire in Hollywood. For the grandson of an immigrant, Joe Kennedy was remarkably intolerant. His anti-semitism would grow through the years, until it became an obsession that helped destroy his promising political career.

He traveled out to Hollywood for the first time in the mid 1920's. There he bought a small film company that churned out "B" movies and cheap westerns. And soon he also got involved in a tempestuous longtime affair with actress Gloria Swanson—not the first or last of his romantic liaisons. For the next two and a half years, he commuted back and forth from California by rail.

Rose Kennedy tried hard to adjust to the situation. Each year she traveled alone to Europe, dividing her time between visiting religious shrines and shopping for designer clothing. At home, she was sometimes emotionally distant—but always highly organized.

Rose put clocks in every room so that the children wouldn't be late for meals. She carefully color-coded the bathing suits worn by her brood. And she got into the habit of pinning notes to her dress to remind her of the day's chores.

Both parents encouraged the children to take an active interest in sports such as sailing, swimming, golf, and tennis. No slackers were allowed. Nor failures.

"We want winners. We don't want losers around here."
JOE SR.

With both parents gone a great deal, the children learned to rely on each other. The older kids clustered together, practising a kind of "rough love" that involved aggressive testing and teasing.

Like his father, Young Joe was tough, sturdy, outgoing, and driven. He was well aware of his position of leadership in the family—and was ready to take on the burden:

"I've got to be an example for a lot of brothers and sisters."

And he wasn't afraid to bully younger brother Jack either. Young Joe taught his underweight sibling to stand up and take punishment. Eventually, Jack learned that it was far better to hit and run. And he also perfected a pointed sarcasm with which to needle his stronger rival.

Jack was born with an unstable back which was constantly being injured. Throughout his youth, he suffered from mysterious blood diseases that sapped his strength. Several times his parents feared he would die. But because he had to spend so much time in bed, JFK became the only member of the family who genuinely liked to read.

Despite his intelligence, Jack did poorly in the private schools he attended as an adolescent. Perhaps his mind was on his health. He drank whole cream to try to put on weight. An attack of what was called a "wasting disease" sent him into the hospital. Classmates were told to pray for his life.

Family members tried to make light about his bad blood condition: If a mosquito bit Jack Kennedy, younger brother Bobby once said, the mosquito would die. Jack himself joked that if someone wrote his biography, it would have to be titled, "John Kennedy: A Medical History."

When he wasn't worrying about his health, he was thinking about his brother. Young Joe, he told everyone at school, played football better, danced better, got better grades. The only thing Jack Kennedy excelled in was making trouble and practical jokes. At one point he was thrown out of school for a prank. It took a visit from his influential father to get him reinstated. Joe Sr. scolded the boy:

"Don't let me lose confidence in you again because it will be pretty near impossible to restore it..."

Despite all the trouble, Jack was voted "most likely to succeed" by his classmates. This surprised almost everyone until it became clear that the youth had fixed the election.

In 1935, Jack entered Princeton, but reoccurring illness forced him to withdraw within the semester. Back in the hospital, tests were inconclusive. He joked that there was nothing wrong with him other than leukemia.

"Took a peek at my chart yesterday and could see that they were mentally measuring me for a coffin."

That summer Jack was well enough to go out West with his older brother to work on a ranch owned by one of his father's wealthy friends. The food and outdoor life agreed with him. That fall John F. Kennedy enrolled at Harvard.

At home, both of the older sons sat at the Big Table with Rose and Joe Sr. Eventually they were joined by Kathleen—nicknamed Kick. The eldest son liked to lock horns with his father, arguing the issues of the day, and even daring to disagree. Jack and Kick, in contrast, tried to avoid direct conflict. They got their way through humor, charm, and cunning.

Robert Kennedy, born in 1925, sat with the children. The runt of the family, he was the odd man out—stuck precariously between the younger and older generation of Kennedy kids. Small, stammering, inarticulate, Bobby somehow always wound up doing things wrong. And there was a serious, even brooding side to him. Of all the brothers, he was the only one with deep religious feelings.

Frustrated that he couldn't swim, Bobby once jumped from a boat into the icy waters off of Cape Cod. It would either be sink or swim. Bobby's hero, Young Joe, leaped in right after to save him. But Jack, typically, stood aloof on the shore, probably wondering whether Bobby was more foolish than brave.

Young Joe's leadership was again confirmed when his parents took the unusual step of making him godfather to the last two members of the family: sister Jean, born in 1928, and Edward, known as Teddy, born in 1932.

It was in that same year that Joseph Kennedy Sr. got personally involved in politics for the first time. The United States was in the midst of the worst economic depression in its history. One quarter of all Americans were unemployed. Millions of farmers were losing their land. And millions of other people around the country were losing their homes. Joe Sr. seriously worried about revolution. Maybe America needed a NEW DEAL.

> "I felt and said I would be willing to part with half of what I had if I could be sure of keeping, under law and order, the other half."

Big Business couldn't deal with the catastrophe. Maybe Big Government could. Kennedy decided to throw his support behind the Democratic candidate for President, Franklin Delano Roosevelt. He explained that he wanted FDR in the White House for his own security and the security of his children.

Joe Sr. provided money to the Roosevelt campaign, served as an advisor, and helped make important alliances for the candidate. But when FDR won, he failed to offer Kennedy an important post in the government.

Joe Sr. demanded back the money he had lent the Democrats and threatened to cause even more trouble. Finally, he was offered a job in the newly formed Securities and Exchange Commission, which would oversee the Stock Market. Critics compared this to appointing the fox to oversee the hen house. Yet Kennedy did an excellent job, and became a trusted Roosevelt associate. But the real pay-off did not come until 1938.

In the Spring of that year, Joseph Kennedy Sr.—the grandson of an Irish farmer—was named American Ambassador to England. FDR hoped that Kennedy's hardnosed pragmatism would help him serve as the White House's eyes and ears in Europe.

With war practically inevitable, Roosevelt needed someone tough enough to see through Hitler's bluff and bluster. Instead, Kennedy seemed to pledge blind allegiance to the cause of peace—at any price. The Ambassador joined those in England who were willing to try to appease the Nazis. This group included the wealthy Astor family, pacifist George Bernard Shaw, and several key leaders of government. It was the biggest mistake of Joseph Kennedy's life

33

Yet things started so well. Soon as they arrived, the Kennedy clan became the hit of London. Prime Minister Neville Chamberlain immediately befriended the new Ambassador. And the family was treated like visiting royalty by both English high society and the press. Young Joe and Jack stayed behind at Harvard, but kept up with the thrilling events.

The English Prime Minister foolishly thought he could handle German militarism. Yet only eleven days after Kennedy's arrival in England, the Nazis risked world war by boldly annexing neighboring Austria. Throughout the crisis, Chamberlain was strangely untroubled. He compared Germany to a boa constrictor, and predicted that Hitler would now have to stop and digest what he'd just swallowed before going after anything else. Kennedy agreed completely.

The Ambassador was also influenced by meeting Charles Lindbergh, who had just returned from Hitler's Germany. The Nazis had rolled out the red carpet for the American aviation hero—the first man to fly the Atlantic. Fellow pilot Hermann Goering, now chief of the German airforce, had even scheduled special aerial demonstrations of the *Luftwaffe's* invincibility. Lindbergh was suitably impressed. And he warned ominously that enemy bombers would level London in the first weeks of any conflict.

Kennedy reported to President Roosevelt that England could never stand up to the Nazis. When FDR seemed to disagree, the Ambassador privately complained that the Jews and the American press were using their influence on FDR to drag America into the coming war with Germany.

The German Ambassador, on the other hand, got along famously with Kennedy. He wired Berlin that according to Kennedy, most Americans didn't seem to mind the Nazi persecution of the Jews, only "the loud clamour with which we accompanied this purpose."

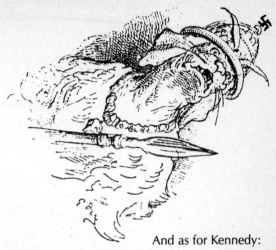

And as for Kennedy:

"He himself understood our Jewish policy completely; he was from Boston and there, in one golf club and in other clubs, no Jews had been admitted for the past 50 years."

In June, the Ambassador's two oldest sons joined him in London. Young Joe had just graduated Harvard. His stated ambition was to become the first Irish Catholic President of the United States—that is, if his father didn't get the job before him.

JFK, on the other hand, was content to stay out of the spotlight. He was more than happy *not* to be the focus of his father's driving ambition. His goal was to become a political writer, perhaps, or a college teacher.

35

Jack's inquisitive mind led him to question many of the things his arch-conservative father took for granted: Fascism, for example, which the Ambassador believed was the antidote to the spread of Communism.

In 1937, JFK had visited Mussolini's Italy and Hitler's Germany. He was infuriated by the Nazis' arrogance and consuming sense of superiority. And he learned of their cruelty by interviewing refugees from the Civil War in Spain—where the Nazis and Fascists were allied with the Franco forces his father supported. Jack came to the conclusion that you simply couldn't get along with dictators by giving into them.

In September of 1938, JFK was proven correct when Hitler again threatened war—this time against the Czechs. Prime Minister Chamberlain shuttled back and forth to Germany, desperately trying to keep the peace. Finally, England caved in completely at the famous conference in Munich.

According to the agreement, Hitler was given the industrialized half of Czechoslovakia without a fight. Chamberlain arrived back in London waving the treaty paper and declaring that he had won "peace in our time."

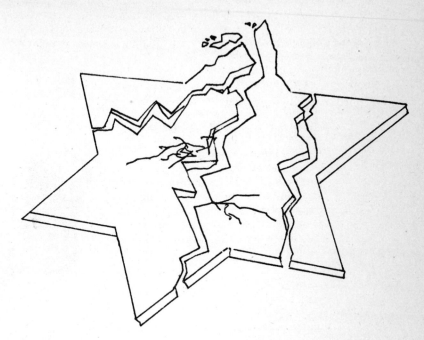

Soon after, Nazi mobs attacked Jews all over Germany, shattering windows, burning synagogues, killing or arresting thousands. This brutal event was called *Kristallnacht*—because of all the broken glass. Previously, Hitler had less dramatically persecuted his many enemies—including Labor leaders, Socialists, Catholics, Fundamentalist Protestants, Jehovah's Witnesses, as well as Jews. But now the civilized world was horrified.

For the Ambassador, however, this event represented an opportunity to create U.S. foreign policy: Since the Jews obviously weren't welcome in Germany, Kennedy offered a plan to ship them all to Africa or somewhere in the Americas. Millions in the United States, including President Roosevelt, were outraged by this capitulation to Nazi injustice.

Then, on September 1, 1939, Hitler could no longer be appeased. German troops launched a full-scale attack on Poland. England and France were committed by Treaty to intervene. Chamberlain vainly tried to get the Nazis to pull back. When they refused, Britain was forced to declare war.

Within a month, Nazi tanks and dive bombers overwhelmed the poorly-armed Poles. The speed of the victory only convinced the Ambassador of the inevitability of English defeat. He told everyone who would listen that it was only a matter of time before the Germans were in London. The only intelligent solution was surrender, followed by an alliance with the Nazis against the Russians.

Winston Churchill, Chamberlain's old rival, was furious. For years he had warned England about the Nazi danger. For his efforts, Kennedy and his Appeasement friends had mocked Churchill as a drunkard and a warmonger. Now Churchill was appointed to England's "War Council." This is what he had to say about the Ambassador's position:

"...I for one would willingly lay down my life in combat rather than, in fear of defeat, surrender to the menaces of these sinister men."

FDR realized that America's security depended on England's will to resist. That's why the President established secret ties with Churchill, months before he became the British Prime Minister. While Kennedy, who Roosevelt no longer trusted, was marked for recall from England at the first possible moment.

Back in the U.S., Young Joe was still carrying out his father's agenda. At Harvard he organized a chapter of *America First*. This organization was led by people like Lindbergh, as well as pacifists and pro-Germans who demanded that the nation follow a strict policy of isolationism. There was no need to fight in Europe, they declared. Fortress America would keep the peace in the hemisphere.

JFK, as usual, followed his own path. In his last year at Harvard he wrote a long paper that described why the English failed to stand up to Hitler. He blamed Chamberlain and other leaders for not "educating" the people about the Nazi threat. Later, Jack's analysis was published as a book called *Why England Slept*. The book was very successful, and its young author quickly began to be noticed.

As America began to mobilize for war, JFK followed brother Joe into the Navy. At first Jack was rejected because of his bad back. He tried to build himself up with a regime of Charles Atlas workout exercises. Finally he got the Ambassador, now cooling his heels in Washington, to pull some strings for him.

By the Fall of 1941, Jack was given a Washington desk job in Naval Intelligence. Just before the Japanese attacked Pearl Harbor, JFK began a romance with Inga Arvad, a beautiful Dane suspected of being a Nazi spy. The FBI bugged her room and recorded Jack discussing his highly classified work between bouts of lovemaking.

When the Ambassador was informed, he used his influence to get his son transferred to active sea duty—and away from Inga. Soon Jack found himself training to take command of one of the fast Patrol Torpedo boats in which he would one day become a hero.

After training, JFK was made a PT boat instructor. And it wasn't until April 1943 that he was actually given command of the PT-109, based on the island of Tulagi, in the South Pacific. Jack was an easy-going, informal skipper. Unlike brother Joe, he felt no particular need to vindicate the family name or achieve some personal glory. He was just excited about finally getting into action.

On August 1, a flotilla of 14 PT boats headed out to meet a squadron of four Japanese destroyers. No action was reported. Returning back to base after sunset, the PT-109 got separated from the other American forces in the area.

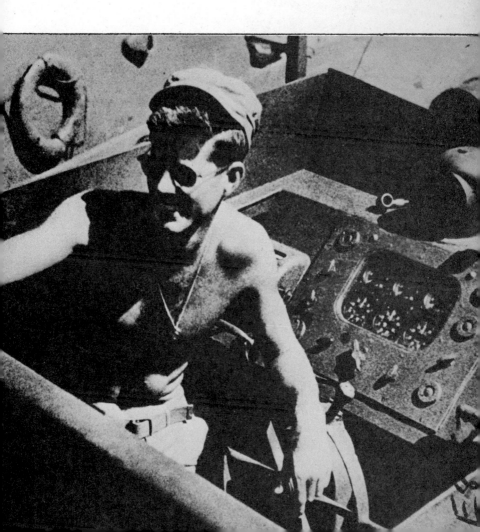

It was 2:30 in the morning of August 2nd. Lt. John F. Kennedy was at the wheel of the PT-109. Many of the men were asleep. Out of the darkness came the towering shadow of a Japanese destroyer, which plowed right into the American craft and quickly cut it in half. At that moment, JFK remembered thinking:

"This is how it feels to be killed."

Two American seamen *were* killed. Another three were badly wounded. Jack swam to one man and dragged him back to the wreckage of the boat. There the survivors clung all night. In the morning they spotted a small island about three miles away. The lieutenant towed one of the wounded men toward land with a rope he held clenched in his teeth.

42

That night, JFK swam out alone to the middle of the strait where his boat went down. All he carried was a pistol that he planned on firing if a rescue ship came by. But when he tried to swim back to shore, he was caught in the tide. Exhausted by swimming, he gave himself up to his fate. And a lucky wave carried him back to land. Next night he went out again.

Four days later the crew of the PT-109 was rescued. News of Jack Kennedy's exploits made the front page of the *New York Times* and other papers around the country.

Young Joe happened to be home on leave in Hyannis when the family heard the news. He was a Navy pilot down in the Caribbean. The mission of his seaplane was to hunt for enemy submarines. So far he was yet to see any action. And here was his kid brother, Jack, already a hero.

Friends noticed that Young Joe sometimes cried when he thought he was alone. Making a fist, he'd swear, "By God, I'll show them." Eventually he did.

Sent to the war zone in England, Young Joe began taking risks. He flew his plane closer and closer to heavy German defenses on the French coast. His crew bitterly complained about the extensive antiaircraft damage they were sustaining.

When Young Joe finished his regular tour of duty, he volunteered for an extra month of missions. On leave, he gambled heavily. Nothing seemed important to him any longer—least of all his life. He seemed fixed on achieving some kind of elusive glory.

44

Just before he was to be sent back home to America, Young Joe volunteered for a final, top secret mission against the V-1 rocket bases the Germans were using to pulverize London. An experienced pilot was needed to pilot a plane loaded with high explosives. As the bomber neared its target, the pilot would switch to a radio control guided by an airman in another plane. Only when radio control was established, could the pilot parachute to safety.

After some training, Joseph Kennedy Jr. was ready. When asked if he wanted to take out some combat insurance, he refused and said, "Nobody in my family needs insurance." Before he boarded his plane, Young Joe phoned a friend of the family with this revealing message:

"...If I don't come back tell my dad...despite our differences—that I love him very much."

On August 13, 1944, the Ambassador was notified that 28 minutes after take-off, an explosion occurred that turned Young Joe's plane into a giant fireball.

Stunned, Joseph Kennedy Sr. walked outside the house onto the beach and told the children the news. He asked them to look after their mother. And then he insisted that they go on with the sailing race that had been planned for the afternoon. Young Joe, he explained, would've wanted it that way.

JFK remembered standing there alone on the sand, watching his father walk slowly back into the house. Jack was thinking that suddenly he was the oldest of the Kennedy children, the heir apparent, the successor. Whether he wanted it or not, it was now his time to perform, his turn to live out his father's ambitions.

Even four months later, JFK confessed that he still felt his father's eyes on the back of his neck.

"When the war is over...I'll be back here with Dad trying to parlay a lost PT boat and a bad back into political advantage...Dad is ready right now and can't understand why Johnny boy isn't all engines full ahead."

At that moment in time, it would've been hard to find a more reluctant candidate for greatness.

Chapter 2: **The President**

"I'm shadow boxing in a match the shadow is always going to win."

JFK

47

The ghost of Young Joe haunted Jack Kennedy in the years after World War II. He realized that his brother's death had brought an end to his precarious freedom. If he now entered politics, his victory would be as his brother's stand-in. But if he lost, the failure would be his alone.

Discharged from the Navy, JFK returned home thin as a rail. His bad back had been aggravated by the ordeal following the sinking of PT 109. Malaria contracted in the South Pacific continued to sap his strength. But the worst was the pressure he was feeling from his father. He complained to a friend, "I'm being fattened up in mind and body." Fattened for the slaughter was what he meant.

"...Dad has decided that he's going to be the ventriloquist, so I guess that leaves me the role of the dummy."

Jack was happy when he could leave for San Francisco, where he attended the founding of the United Nations as a reporter for the Hearst newspaper chain. There he met many of the top newsmen in the country, and became fascinated by the way they helped to form public opinion. All his life he maintained a keen interest in the men and women who reported the news.

In 1946 Jack couldn't hold out any longer. At his father's urging, he decided to run for U.S. Congress. The district was in Boston, a place Kennedy hadn't lived in since he was nine. He was immediately attacked as a carpetbagger, a rich outsider who wanted to buy a seat for himself in government. There were eight others in the race.

Jack insisted on running a new kind of campaign. He recruited friends from college and men he'd served with in the Navy. As much as possible, he avoided the old guard of cigar-chewing ward politicians that his father had grown up with. Kennedy's slogan was:

THE NEW GENERATION OFFERS A LEADER

The Ambassador still operated from the sidelines. In his mind, Jack was going to need all the help he could get. The boy didn't have the right temperament for politics. Much too stiff, too reserved, too much of a gentleman. He didn't like shaking hands or rubbing shoulders with people. But JFK learned fast.

He became a tireless campaigner. Early in the morning he was out introducing himself to the voters—and actually shaking their hands. All day he went door to door, passing out brochures. Nights he spent speaking at rallies, attending political house parties, and planning strategy for the next morning.

Slowly, Jack Kennedy began to meet the real people of Boston, middleclass and poor, from whom he'd always been sheltered. More than once, the candidate had to be dragged away from a conversation with a local worker or veteran. The real concerns of voters in his district suddenly began showing up in his speeches—which also ceased to be so nervous and choppy.

Towards election day, the polls showed JFK ahead of all the other candidates. The Ambassador, who funded the campaign, seemed unimpressed:

"With what I'm spending I could elect my chauffeur."

50

$\mathbf{Y}$et Joe Sr. *was* impressed when his son actually scored more votes than all the other candidates combined. He told a friend he would've given 5000:1 odds against it ever happening.

JFK began his career in government by showing up late for his first day in Congress. Usually he wore the first things he found: wrinkled khakis, rumpled sports jackets, and gravy spotted ties. It was almost as if he was saying he didn't give a damn, that he was just going through the motions. "If you don't want to work for a living," he once joked, "this is as good a job as any."

It was hard for Jack to get excited about anything. He was moved to take a stand on just a few issues: new housing for veterans, for example, and the Marshall Plan for rebuilding Europe. On the first point, JFK wound up attacking the powerful American Legion, which opposed government aid to housing. On the second, he defied an even more dangerous foe—his father.

The Ambassador insisted that America would go broke helping Europe heal itself from the War. JFK feared that a weak Europe would fall into Joseph Stalin's greedy hands. Eventually, the son had to take a stand:

"Now look here, Dad, you have your political views and I have mine. I'm going to vote the way I feel I must on this..."

51

In 1948, the tragic death of his sister Kathleen in an aircrash shocked him deeply. Jack began to be preoccupied by thoughts of his own mortality. Eventually his chronic illness was diagnosed as Addison's Disease, a malfunction of the adrenal gland that left him weak and open to infection. His back continued to hurt him, but the Addison's Disease made further operations highly dangerous. He received *steroid* implants which helped a little. Yet there was no real cure for his condition. He just had to live with it— that is, if he was lucky.

In 1951 Congressman Kennedy took a fact finding tour to Israel and the Far East. It was one of the turning points in his life. On this trip Jack brought along his brother Robert, someone he barely knew.

Bobby, as everyone called him, seemed silent and serious. The least athletic of the Kennedy boys, he worked hard to toughen himself up. After serving in the Navy as a seaman, Bobby enrolled at Harvard. There he joined the football team, and played more than once with a dislocated shoulder or broken bone. Part of him seemed to relish testing himself. No great student, Bobby finally went on to graduate Law School by "sheer persistence."

On the crucial trip to the Far East, Jack learned to value his brother's ability to focus on a situation and identify with the people involved. The brothers quickly learned to be friends. And both were deeply affected by what they found in the underdeveloped Third World.

52

Here in Asia millions were struggling against colonialism, poverty, and disease. Communism was on the march. Mao Ze Dong had already taken control of China. The North Koreans had just invaded the South. And guerrilla wars were springing up everywhere.

India's Prime Minister Nehru met with the two young Americans. Nehru had been a close friend of Mahatma Gandhi. Together they had peacefully led India to freedom. Now, Nehru said that Communism was winning around the world because it seemed to offer people ideas that were worth dying for. Bobby realized that the West would have to do the same:

"We only have status quo to offer these people. Commies can offer a change."

In Indochina, the French were desperately trying to hold on to their colonies: Laos, Cambodia, and most important of all, Vietnam. From the US Embassy in Saigon, Jack could watch the nightly battle just outside the city between the colonial army and the Vietnamese guerrillas led by Ho Chi Minh. The Era of Empire was over, he realized. And the United States better not forget it.

Returning to America, JFK made up his mind to run for the Senate. His opponent was the popular Republican, Henry Cabot Lodge Jr., son of Honey Fitz' old enemy. Political experts told Jack to wait, that he was still young. Kennedy knew better. His health was faltering. In Japan he been hospitalized with a temperature of 106 degrees. Somehow he survived. But maybe next time he wouldn't.

"I can't wait. I don't have time. I've got to do it *now*!"

Throughout Massachusetts, hundreds of Kennedy volunteers were ready to begin the campaign. Yet Jack refused to involve himself with the nitty gritty, day-to-day decisions that matter in a close campaign. Precious months slipped by. The campaign was grinding to a stop.

J oe Kennedy Sr. stepped in to fill the vacuum. The Ambassador immediately began to involve all the old politicos his son had tried to avoid. A desperate message went out to Bobby from Kenny O'Donnell, one of Jack's campaign managers: To avoid a catastrophe, the Ambassador had to be removed. Bobby reluctantly left a job at the Justice Department and took control. One of his first orders was:

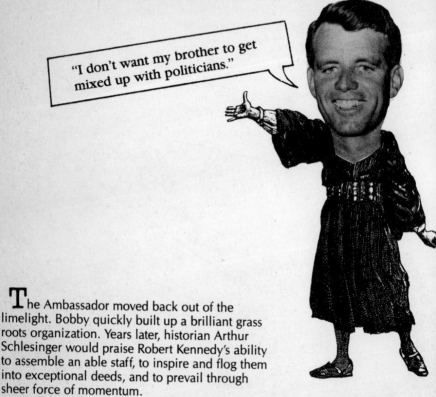

"I don't want my brother to get mixed up with politicians."

T he Ambassador moved back out of the limelight. Bobby quickly built up a brilliant grass roots organization. Years later, historian Arthur Schlesinger would praise Robert Kennedy's ability to assemble an able staff, to inspire and flog them into exceptional deeds, and to prevail through sheer force of momentum.

Once in motion, Jack campaigned hard. His back trouble reduced him to using crutches to walk—whenever he couldn't be seen by the public. His mother and sisters helped by throwing Kennedy Teas, which were attended by thousands of women around the state. Events like this added to the glamor of the candidate who was still remembered for his wartime heroism.

On election day, Jack triumphed with 51 percent of the vote.

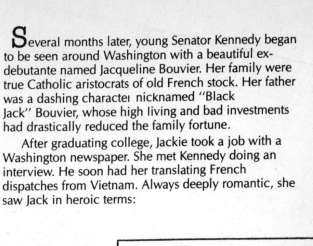

Several months later, young Senator Kennedy began to be seen around Washington with a beautiful ex-debutante named Jacqueline Bouvier. Her family were true Catholic aristocrats of old French stock. Her father was a dashing character nicknamed "Black Jack" Bouvier, whose high living and bad investments had drastically reduced the family fortune.

After graduating college, Jackie took a job with a Washington newspaper. She met Kennedy doing an interview. He soon had her translating French dispatches from Vietnam. Always deeply romantic, she saw Jack in heroic terms:

"You must think of him as this little boy, sick so much of the time, reading in bed, reading history, reading the Knights of the Round Table..."

Jack and Jackie had more in common than just their names. "Both had the ability to make you feel that there was no place on earth you'd rather be than sitting there in intimate conversation with them," recalled Lem Billings, one of Kennedy's oldest friends. Jack loved to watch her charm at work.

Jackie was intelligent and highly cultured. But like most of the Kennedy women, she had little interest in politics. At this point in his career, that was fine with Jack. The couple married in the summer of 1953.

The following year, JFK began to a make a name on the national scene. His talent was for speaking out on the issues—not for getting laws passed. Jack believed, perhaps naively, in the power of ideas. He had no patience for the methodical wheeling and dealing that builds working majorities. He preferred the role of the Lone Ranger.

In domestic affairs, he repeatedly attacked racial discrimination on the job. He spoke out for a higher minimum wage for workers. And he took a stand against corruption in labor unions, even though it probably cost him votes at home.

Yet it was on the international front that JFK staked claim to leadership. His ideas had continued to evolve over the years since he'd left his father's home. For ultra-conservatives like Joseph Kennedy, the world was viewed as a battlefield between the Evil Empire of Communism and the *freedom-loving West*. Revolutions were something exported by Moscow, like caviar. The local situation mattered little.

59

Jack's view was more complex. Revolutions, he believed, were caused by "revolutionary conditions" such as poverty, hunger, and oppression. America had to offer the world a real alternative to misery. Not only must the rich nations of the West share part of their wealth with the poor. But even at home, Americans must learn to help each other:

"If we lack compassion for those who are sick or poor or aged, we cannot convincingly show such compassion abroad. We cannot identify ourselves with the hundreds of millions...who fight not only Communism but also misery, ignorance, starvation, disease."

JFK practiced what he preached when he opposed massive military aid to South America. The region, he felt, was not directly threatened by Soviet power. The money would be better spent by providing technical assistance to the starving peoples south of the border.

And in Asia, he attacked France's futile attempt to cling to its Indochinese colonies. In Vietnam, Ho Chi Minh's forces had trapped a large French army at a place called Dien Bien Phu. President Dwight Eisenhower, a Republican, was considering a U.S. air strike against the rebels, as well as hundreds of millions in additional military aid. "The time has come for the American people to be told the truth about Indochina."—JFK

Kennedy opposed US assistance unless the money was used "to encourage through all means available the freedom and independence" Asians were fighting for. He also told the nation that no amount of U.S. aid could "conquer an enemy which is everywhere and at the same time nowhere." Nearly a decade later, he would come to the same conclusion about his own failed policies in Vietnam.

JFK's health again began to deteriorate. His weight dropped from 180 pounds to only 140. The doctors said he needed surgery on his back. But Jack knew that his Addison's disease made any operation life threatening. Still, what choice did he have?

"I'd rather be dead than spend the rest of my life on these goddamned crutches."

While in the hospital, JFK missed the important vote to censure notorious Senator Joseph McCarthy—a man who'd made a career out of hunting Communists. This was one fight he was happy to avoid.

62

Like Jack, Joe McCarthy entered government right after World War II. A fellow Catholic, he was befriended by the whole Kennedy clan—especially the arch-conservative Ambassador. McCarthy even dated Jack's sister Eunice. Like most of the young men who'd been veterans, McCarthy complained that America won the war but we were losing the peace to the Soviets. The only explanation was cowardice or TREASON.

McCarthy's Senate investigations were supposed to uncover the network of Communist subversives in America. Together with the Red Hunters of the House Un-American Activities Committee (HUAC), the search started with government, but soon spread to labor unions, school teachers, writers, and even actors. Everyone was suspect.

McCarthy and his assistant, Roy Cohn, helped create a cruel, circus atmosphere in the hearings with wild accusations, smears and innuendos. Witnesses were attacked for their sexual preferences or for attending suspicious meetings twenty years before. Guilt by association was the rule. To prove innocence, witnesses had to "name names", and implicate others. Hundreds of lives were ruined on the basis of heresay alone. And those who dared oppose McCarthy's methods could expect to have their own patriotism questioned.

Robert Kennedy, unfortunately, had gotten involved in this inquisition. The Ambassador used his anti-Communist connections to get his son a job as assistant counsel on McCarthy's committee. Yet after only few months, Bobby was disgusted enough to walk out of the hearings in protest. Eventually he joined the Democrats who were opposing McCarthy.

Privately, Jack was angered and deeply embarrassed by his former friend. But publicly, he felt he had to stay silent: "How could I demand that Joe McCarthy be censured for things he did when my brother was on his staff?"

Family loyalty was too strong. The Senate's censure broke McCarthy's power forever. But in years to come, liberals would always remember that Kennedy was the only Democrat in the Senate who failed to vote against the witch hunt. And it would cost him dearly when he made his first try for national office.

JFK's back operation almost cost him his life as well. At one point, a priest was summoned to give him the last rites. It took months to recover. While he lay in a hospital bed with a hole in his back as big as a fist, Jack had lots of time to think about courage. Winston Churchill, one of his heroes, had plenty of it. But there were also many American leaders of the past who had stood up for unpopular causes—at the risk of their careers and sometimes their lives.

The result of such thinking was a book called *Profiles In Courage*. Jack wrote this short collection of political biographies while still in his hospital bed. When *Profiles* was awarded the Pulitzer Prize the following year, Jack found himself thrust into the national spotlight again—this time as one of the intellectual leaders of the Democratic Party.

The operation was ultimately a success. Together with regular novocaine injections and cortisone pills, Jack could function without pain for the first time in years.

His attitude changed too. "Jack had grown up thinking he was doomed," good friend Lem Billings recalled. "Now he had a different view. Instead of thinking he was doomed, he thought he was lucky."

HERE'S LUCK!

His luck continued. In 1956, JFK was asked to give the nominating speech for the Democratic candidate for President, Adlai Stevenson. At the convention, Jack found himself suddenly being championed as a possible candidate for Vice President.

Not everyone was in favor, of course. Southerners warned that a Catholic candidate would only lose votes in their part of the country. Liberal Democrats attacked Kennedy for showing "too much profile, not enough courage," especially in regard to Joe McCarthy. They were fiercely against Kennedy appearing on the ticket.

For once, Ambassador Kennedy found himself on the same side as the liberals. He loudly forbade Jack to pursue the nomination. President Eisenhower was far too popular. Stevenson, who was viewed as a university "egghead," would surely lose and lose big. And when that happened, Joe Sr. warned, they would all blame you.

Jack, as usual, followed his own course. For two days he politicked heavily and came within just a few votes of getting the nomination. He lost out—and Kennedys hated to lose. But he gained something in return.

"I've learned that you don't get far in politics until you become a total politician."

65

That meant dealing with the leaders of the Democratic Party, as well as the voters. No longer could he play the Lone Ranger. He had to join the team. That is—until he could make sure that the team joined him.

Throughout New England, Jack gave speeches for Stevenson. Bobby joined the campaign organization to learn how to run a national race—or how not to run it. He reported back that Adlai's approach was all wrong, too intellectual. "You'd never believe it," Bobby said. "He gives an elaborate speech on world affairs to a group of twenty-five coal miners standing on a railroad track in West Virginia."

When President Eisenhower again triumphed over Stevenson, JFK realized that the road to the Presidency was clear. He began cementing relationships with big city political bosses like Richard Daley of Chicago, who could help deliver votes. And to protect his sons, Ambassador Kennedy stepped even further back into the shadows:

"I don't want them to inherit my enemies. It's tough enough they inherit my friends."

66

Bobby was soon making enemies of his own. He took a job with a Senate Committee investigating labor corruption. His main target was the leader of the powerful Teamsters' Union, Jimmy Hoffa. Unlike the Kennedys, Hoffa had come up the hard way. He was rough, ruthless, and very resourceful.

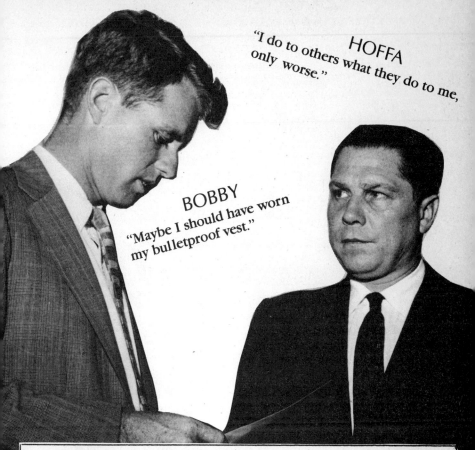

HOFFA

"I do to others what they do to me, only worse."

BOBBY

"Maybe I should have worn my bulletproof vest."

Bobby confidently took control of the investigation. It was the first time in his life that he was his own man—not an extension of his father or his brother. As the case developed Bobby swore that if Hoffa wasn't convicted, "I'll jump off the Capitol."

But the Teamster boss was a tough nut to crack. His ties to organized crime were well disguised. And his henchmen kept quiet; they were obviously more afraid of their boss than they were of the Feds. When it was Hoffa's turn to testify, he showed that he also could keep his lip buttoned:

"To the best of my recollection, I must recall in my memory, I cannot remember."

Bobby was disappointed when Hoffa squirmed out of the case. He partly blamed the F.B.I., which was so focused on Communism that it was no help in the fight against crime.

Meanwhile, Jack continued to speak out for a more realistic approach to the problems of the world. He demanded that France grant independence to its large North African colony, Algeria. Here a bloody war of liberation was intensifying. And JFK feared that a long struggle would tear France apart and weaken the Western alliance.

President Eisenhower attacked Kennedy for his interference. But within a year, French leader Charles de Gaulle announced his own plans to free the colony.

Kennedy was on a roll. He began to talk about a dynamic new strategy to deal with the world:

"What we must offer is a revolution— a political and social revolution far superior to anything the Communists can offer."

68

It was a fresh solution, vigorous, just, and positive. People started listening. By 1960, Jack was probably the most popular Democrat in America, and the likely candidate for President. But there were still some obstacles in his path. Some people worried:

Was JFK too young to be President? Were liberals ready to support him?

Was America ready to vote for a Catholic? In reality, this was the most important question of all. The last Catholic who ran for President was Al Smith. And he was badly defeated in the year 1928. Would it be any different with Kennedy?

JFK's main opponents were Hubert Humphrey, the darling of the liberals...

And a shrewd Texas politician by the name of Lyndon Johnson.

Humphrey, Senator from Minnesota, had suffered a big loss in the primaries when JFK swept neighboring Wisconsin. Johnson threw his support behind Humphrey in a desperate attempt to stop Kennedy.

The final battleground was little West Virginia: a poor, mountainous border state, mostly populated by small farmers and coal miners. Only 5 percent of its people were Catholic. Many of the rest were hardcore Fundamentalist Protestants who feared that a Catholic President would be a puppet of the Pope in Rome.

JFK had been warned not to make a fight here. Why risk bringing up the religious issue in a hostile place with so few votes? Kennedy could easily give up the state to Humphrey and still win the nomination. But Jack decided to take the risk. Sooner or later, he knew he would have to face the religious question.

And he knew how he would answer:

"Nobody asked me if I was a Catholic when I joined the United States Navy. Nobody asked my brother if he was a Catholic or Protestant before he climbed into an American bomber plane to fly his last mission."

Arriving in West Virginia, he told a crowd that every President takes a solemn oath to protect the Constitution and the separation of Church and State. If he breaks his oath, he is not only guilty of an impeachable crime against the law. But he is also committing a sin against God.

Jack carried this message back and forth across the state in the private airplane his father bought, The Caroline— named after JFK's two year old daughter.

And it was here, in the slums of the mine towns and the shacks along the country roads of West Virginia, that Kennedy first discovered the extent of poverty in America. He was outraged and sickened by what he saw. How could the richest country on earth let its people live like this? A new commitment to the poor and powerless began to enter his speeches.

The people of West Virginia quickly responded to Kennedy's call for social justice. They were aware of the advantage his father's wealth gave him. But they admired Jack's courage in risking the religious issue. In the end, they also gave the young Senator their votes.

At the Democratic Convention in Los Angeles, JFK won the nomination on the first ballot. He eloquently set the theme of the campaign by declaring that all Americans stood on the edge of a New Frontier, the frontier of the 1960s:

"Beyond that frontier are areas of science and space, unsolved problems of peace and war, unconquered pockets of ignorance and prejudice, unanswered questions of poverty and surplus...I am asking each of you to be new pioneers on that new frontier."

The liberal wing of the party still had their doubts. One Convention delegate complained:

"It isn't what Kennedy believes that worries me. It's whether he believes anything."

Kennedy was proud that he was still his own man, neither a card-carrying liberal or conservative. He was, in his own words, "a realist." He started with the questions, not the answers. And that meant he felt free to make the best possible decisions based on the facts—not on ideology. His choice for Vice President proved that.

JFK wanted a man who could bring "balance" to the ticket: a Protestant, from the South or West, a moderate conservative skilled at wheeling and dealing with the Congress to get laws passed. After an agonizing process of deliberation, he chose his old rival, LYNDON BAINES JOHNSON.

"From here on, LBJ means Let's Back Jack."
—LBJ

But the Northern liberals hated Johnson. To keep them from revolting, Jack made this ominous prediction:

"I'm forty-three years old and I'm the healthiest candidate for President...I'm not going to die in office."

The following month, the Republicans nominated Richard Nixon for President. Nixon had served for eight years as Vice President under Eisenhower. Though he lacked Kennedy's charisma, he was considered a shrewd, tough campaigner. Jack knew he had an uphill fight all the way to the election.

So he went on the attack. He accused the Eisenhower/Nixon Administration of letting America slip behind in science and technology. The Russians, after all, were first to launch a satellite into space—Sputnik.

Kennedy claimed we'd also fallen behind militarily, that we suffered a "missile gap" that the Soviets could exploit. This turned out to be campaign rhetoric, but it did make him seem tougher on the Soviets than Nixon, the career anti-Communist.

And Jack also criticized Eisenhower's relaxed management style. In contrast, he promised to be an active, involved leader. A leader who would revive the economy. Who would include the American people in important decisions. And most important of all, a leader who would make sure that the poor and powerless had a friend in the White House.

Nixon was forced to defend the Eisenhower record. On the crucial religious issue, Nixon deplored any attempt to bring JFK's faith into the election. And he deplored it as often and as vocally as possible.

In Texas, Kennedy "...spoke out to a hostile group of Protestant ministers."

He tamed the audience by declaring, "I am not the Catholic candidate for President. I am the Democratic Party's candidate for President, who happens to be Catholic." Some Protestants began to get the message.

75

Then came the final test: the first televised Presidential Debates. Here the medium was truly the message. Kennedy did not look too young to be President —he looked strong, alert, virile. Nixon, in contrast, was sweating. He had a five o'clock shadow on his jowls. His movements seemed jerky, unconnected with his words.

In front of the 70 million Americans who watched the debate, Kennedy restated his commitment to racial equality. He attacked the many ways blacks were still being held back in this country, and declared:

"We can do better."

That became the underlying message of the Kennedy campaign. In every area, we as Americans could and *should* be doing better.

The very next day, Jack began to be mobbed by fans wherever he went. There were three other televised debates, but they only confirmed Kennedy's appeal. Polls now showed that both candidates were neck and neck. Even Bobby Kennedy, who ran the campaign, wasn't sure how it would turn out.

Then something happened down in the state of Georgia, something which would help change things in America forever. Like most parts of the South in those days, Georgia was a place where racial segregation was still the rule. If you were black, the Civil War had to be fought every day.

A few weeks before the election, 52 black people were arrested for trying to get served at a whites-only restaurant in Atlanta, the capital. Just one man out of the group, a minister, was held and later convicted of the crime of "trespassing." He was sentenced to four months at hard labor at a remote prison farm. Friends and family rightly feared for his life.

Today we know that lone prisoner as the foremost leader of the Civil Rights movement, a Nobel Peace Prize winner, and an eloquent spokesman for nonviolence. His name, of course, was Dr. Martin Luther King.

Vice President Nixon was advised to intervene, but he kept silent. JFK, on the other hand, immediately phoned Dr. King's wife, Coretta. They spoke for only a few moments, but Kennedy made his support clear. Later he told the press:

"She is a friend of mine and I was concerned about the situation."

Bobby followed up with a phone call to the judge in the case—who ordered Dr. King released.

On election day, millions of blacks throughout the country remembered Kennedy's daring act of support. Their votes may have made the difference in states like Texas and Illinois, where the race was too close to call.

Immediate political impact aside, this event had even broader meaning: JFK pushed the whole issue of equality to the front of the nation's agenda. In return, Dr. King furnished Kennedy with a sense of righteousness and moral urgency. No Presidential candidate since Abraham Lincoln had dared to link his fortunes so closely to the cause of freedom. Black America would finally have a friend in the White House.

On election day, Kennedy's campaign team was still worried. The religious issue had never really gone away. In past days, Right Wing conservative organizations had blanketed 20 million homes with vicious anti-Catholic brochures and hate sheets. Polls showed JFK slightly ahead. But the Nixon forces were not about to give up. For as one Republican leader put it:

"I have a deep and abiding faith in the fundamental bigotry of the American people."

John F. Kennedy had another kind of faith. As the votes started rolling in, one of the TV networks predicted that Nixon would win in a landslide. Jack ignored it. An hour later, they reversed their prediction. JFK piled up an early lead in the Northeast. But as the night went on, Nixon started coming on strong in the South and Midwest.

It was not over until 5:45 in the morning, when Secret Service agents suddenly surrounded the Kennedy compound in Hyannis Port. Towards noon, Nixon finally conceded.

Kennedy's margin of victory was ridiculously small: less than 120,000 votes out of 69 million. He did much better in electoral votes, respectably beating Nixon 303-219. Still, JFK couldn't afford to kid himself. He was entering office without a clear mandate from the American people. And he would have to be very careful, especially in the beginning.

For his Cabinet, Kennedy reached out to all sectors of America. His Secretary of Treasury, Douglas Dillon, was an Eisenhower Republican. Robert McNamara, named Secretary of Defense, had been head of Ford Motors. JFK's pick for Secretary of State, Dean Rusk, was formerly the head of the Rockefeller Foundation. And in the United Nations, Kennedy chose Adlai Stevenson, champion of the liberals. Even Harvard historian Arthur Schlesinger got a post as Special Assistant—in effect, he was the White House's Ambassador to Academia.

The only controversial appointment was for Attorney General, the highest law enforcement officer in the land and the President's right hand man. Jack gave this post to the only person he had learned to trust absolutely: Bobby Kennedy. When critics complained that the President's younger brother lacked the necessary experience for the job, JFK replied with some of the wit he would soon display as President:

"I don't see what's wrong with giving Bobby a little experience before he starts to practice law."

Just days after Thanksgiving, the Kennedy clan got another member: John F. Kennedy Jr. Soon the nation was calling the newborn boy "John John." He and his sister Caroline were the first small children to inhabit the White House in decades. At last, America's First Family would actually be a family.

On January 20, 1961, Jack Kennedy rode to his Inauguration, accompanied by departing President Eisenhower. The symbolism was perfect: the oldest President handing power over to the youngest ever elected.

Robert Frost, a New Englander like JFK, was asked to recite a poem at the ceremony. This was intended to celebrate the beginning of what Kennedy hoped would become "a golden age of poetry and power."

Finally, there was John F. Kennedy himself, newly sworn in as President of the United States. His Inaugural Speech is as stirring and memorable today as when it was first spoken, decades ago, on that clear winter morning:

"Let the word go forth from this time and place, to friend and foe alike, that the torch has been passed to a new generation...

"And so, my fellow Americans, ask not what your country can do for you; ask what you can do for your country."

83

Tens of millions in the United States heard this challenge on the television and over the radio. In days to come, many of them—especially the young—would be motivated to new levels of idealism and action.

Yet perhaps the person most moved at that moment was sitting not far from the new President. This man, who was despised as much as he was feared or admired, wore the same formal clothing he had donned over 20 years before when he presented his credentials to the King of England. Feelings of deep satisfaction, mixed with loss, must have flooded his mind at that time. Only days before, he had acknowledged:

"Jack doesn't belong to a family. He belongs to the country."

freedom

85

For Joseph Kennedy Sr., the struggle that had begun a century earlier with a penniless immigrant arriving in America had finally come to an end. The New Frontier, however, was only just beginning.

Chapter 3: **The World In Crisis**

He believed that a great leader should use his power like an artist, skillfully shaping the public support needed to govern. That's what Lincoln and Franklin D. Roosevelt had done. And that's what JFK would also try to do.

In the 1930s FDR had used the new medium of radio to reassure the nation during the bleakest period of the Great Depression. Now Jack Kennedy would try to master the possibilities of television to unite the nation behind him.

He was the first President with the confidence to hold live TV press conferences. There he was able to demonstrate his spontaneous wit and intelligence—as well as his openness to criticism. But to help set the national agenda, JFK found himself relying more and more on formal televised speeches.

Kennedy's Inaugural Address, for example, focused almost entirely on foreign affairs. This was no accident. His heroic vision of America needed a large international stage. And JFK also realized that successes abroad would increase his prestige and power at home. The two were connected. Yet the new President quickly learned that there was one sobering distinction between national and international politics:

"The big difference is between a bill being defeated and the country being wiped out."

A half dozen foreign crises were waiting to break the moment that he sat down in the Oval Office. On practically every continent there was suddenly war, revolution, or bloody repression: the Congo, Angola, Tunisia, Laos, Korea, and the Dominican Republic. And the Russians were threatening to intervene in more than one of them.

All the policy failures of the Eisenhower Administration were now coming back to haunt America. It was as if while moving into the White House, Kennedy found the roof falling in and all the doors blowing off.

JFK looked out at the world and tried to define his strategy for the future. "Our goal is to again influence history," he declared, "instead of merely observing it." Could the United States regain the initiative around the world? Or would the Soviets and their friends carry out Premier Nikita Khrushchev's recent threat:

"**We will bury you.**"

Kennedy's whole upbringing stressed the importance of active competition. He believed it brought out the best in a person or a people. But the problem was: How do you compete with the Communists—without blowing up the world?

The situation in Europe was static. East and West faced each other along a long Iron Curtain that stretched from Scandinavia to the Balkans.

Yet out beyond the Cold War—in the new nations of Africa, Asia, and the Americas—lived nearly half the people on earth. Most of them shared a legacy of poverty, hunger, disease, illiteracy, and oppression. Here, in what we today call the Third World, JFK saw America's greatest challenge.

The main problems facing these people, he insisted, "are not susceptible to a military solution." As President, he intended to compete on social, economic, and ideological grounds. It came down to this: US or USSR— which system offered the best model for development?

"Which society is the most productive? Which society educates its children better?... Which society produces more cultural and intellectual stimulus? Which society, in other words, is the happiest?"

Yet JFK's first major confrontation with the Third World *was* military. And it happened, in fact, only ninety miles away in...

CUBA.

In 1959, guerrillas led by Fidel Castro overthrew the island's corrupt dictator, Fulgencio Batista—who had long been supported by the US government. Cuba's economy was dominated by American corporations and a handful of rich families. Millions lacked adequate food, homes, medical care, or education. Shortly after victory, the Fidelistas began nationalizing big plantations, factories, and resort hotels. *Yanqui* businessmen angrily protested in Washington. And Castro began to fear the inevitable US reaction.

From the Eisenhower White House, it clearly looked like Cuba was turning into an armed Soviet satellite. Ike was outraged that Castro would dare expropriate American property. And now Russian military and economic aid was pouring into Havana. But there were other problems too.

Soon after victory, Castro began to tighten the screws in Cuba, closing the free press and clamping down on the opposition. Revolutionary courts carried out the execution of former Batista supporters—with little or no due process. The whole country seemed on the verge of becoming a one party state with a powerful secret police based on the Communist model.

Ike finally gave his ok to a secret invasion of the island—controlled by the Central Intelligence Agency (CIA), but carried out by Cuban emigres. In the beginning, the plan was for a small "quiet" landing in a mountainous area of the island, where anti-Castro guerrillas could operate effectively. If they were successful, there was even talk of diplomatic recognition.

But soon the operation became a monster. Three or four times as many troops were now involved. Air support was required. And because larger transport ships would be used, the landing zone was changed to a broad marshy area more than 50 miles away from the mountains. On American maps this place was called the BAY OF PIGS.

JFK only learned about the plan—but not all the details—shortly before the election. Once in the White House, the new President began *mañana* the invasion for months. Not because he distrusted the CIA:

"...You always assume that the military and intelligence people have some secret skill not available to ordinary mortals."

94

And not because he didn't want to get rid of Castro. He did. Kennedy justified it by asking why America should "protect" Castro from fellow Cubans who wanted to overthrow him for selling democracy out to the Russians? The truth was that JFK simply didn't want the US caught invading yet another Latin American country.

Reluctantly, Jack gave his OK. On April 17, 1961, several World War II bombers supplied by the CIA attacked Castro's airfields—but were able to destroy only a few planes on the ground. The airstrike was soon followed by the landing of fifteen hundred anti-Castro Cubans at the Bay of Pigs.

Despite CIA assurances, there was no mass anti-Castro uprising in the cities to coincide with the landing. Beset by doubts, President Kennedy refused to order a second air strike. Cuban planes now dominated the air. And within hours, 25,000 Fidelistas had surrounded the beachhead.

It was a complete disaster. The invasion force was quickly forced to surrender. Kennedy was in shock. And he held himself—as Commander in Chief—totally responsible:

"All my life I've known better than to depend on the experts. How could I have been so stupid, to let them go ahead?"

Yet even before the dust settled, Kennedy was plunged into another crisis—this time half way around the world in a tiny, backward corner of Indochina called Laos. Here two Armies vied for power. The pro-Communist Pathet Lao was rapidly advancing towards the capital city of Vientiane. The Royal Laotian Army, supported by America, was simply melting away and refusing to fight.

Could military aid reverse the situation? The Eisenhower Administration had already spent $300 million and the Army they created was practically worthless. Should direct military intervention be considered? Kennedy's military advisors were still furious about the President's refusal to fight at the Bay of Pigs. Now they were insisting that the Pentagon airlift 60,000 US troops to the landlocked country.

This time JFK didn't just go along with the experts. He kept asking hard questions, such as: What if the troops were attacked at the airstrip before they were in position? The Generals had only one solution: use nuclear weapons.

Kennedy knew there had to be another solution: a political one. Against the advice of the military and his more conservative advisors, JFK proposed a coalition government for Laos which would include the Pathet Lao.

This compromise would have been unthinkable during the Eisenhower Administration. Ike feared that any country with a coalition government would eventually go Communist. And he felt there was something immoral about a country that stayed neutral, non-aligned, and accepted aid from the US and the USSR at the same time.

Neutrality is a No-No

EISENHOWER

JFK

But the new President was more inclined to let the nations of the Third World make their own policy. And he realized that half a loaf is sometimes better than no loaf. Or a radioactive one. The Pathet Lao ultimately accepted the deal and a tenuous peace fell on the area.

Suddenly, the world picture deceptively seemed to get brighter. Soviet Premier Nikita Khrushchev offered to meet Kennedy at a summit held in Vienna. JFK hoped that a shining diplomatic victory would overshadow his defeat at the Bay of Pigs. Instead he found out the Russian bear was a lot like his father, "all take and no give."

The two world leaders met in June, 1961. The Soviet chief was a tough political foe who had climbed the bloody ladder to power under Stalin. In 1956, Khrushchev hadn't hesitated to send in Russian tanks to crush a popular uprising in Hungary. Now, the Premier tried to bully the young President, who obviously lacked the will to use similar American force at the Bay of Pigs.

Khrushchev told JFK that the Soviets would continue to support revolutions around the world. He called them "holy wars," and predicted that the nations of the Third World would fall into his hands like rotten apples. Worse, the Soviet leader threatened the freedom of West Berlin—which the US, England, and France were committed to defend.

Returning from Vienna, Kennedy predicted it was going to be "a long cold winter." Berlin was over a hundred miles inside Communist East Germany. The Soviets could easily block the roads leading in from the West. JFK wondered if the West was ready to go head to head with the Red Army.

There could be no negotiated settlement concerning the freedom of Berlin. This was not Laos, where America could afford to compromise. Whatever the risk, Kennedy had to stop any Soviet move against the city. But he also had to resist pushing Khrushchev into a corner. After deliberation, he decided on an oblique, *psychological* response: His weapon was the mass media.

Surrounded by flags, a grim President Kennedy spoke on television about Berlin and the threat to peace in a nuclear age. He announced he was increasing the military budget, asking Congress for authority to call up the Reserves, tripling the size of the Draft, and bolstering US defense forces in Berlin. Then—before he finished—JFK encouraged greater Civil Defense measures, including fallout shelters. He assured the nation:

"We seek peace, but we shall not surrender."

That was it. No ultimatum. Just a somber warning about the dangers of miscalculation. The young President hoped that Khrushchev would get the message.

Tensions steadily continued to rise. Then, on the morning of August 13, Khrushchev made a move that surprised everyone. Though he'd obviously gotten Kennedy's message, his reaction was totally unexpected. Rather than try to keep the West out of Berlin—Khrushchev threw up a wall to keep the East in. Millions of East Germans had already escaped to freedom in the western part of the city. That flood was now stopped by the barbed wire and stone of the Berlin Wall.

The immediate crisis was defused. And although Khrushchev was blocked from carrying out his threat against West Berlin, the Wall helped him to save face in his own Central Committee. Officially, the situation was a draw. But the two superpowers continued their deadly dance.

Meanwhile, the US situation in Indochina was worsening. Laos was stable. But guerrilla warfare was intensifying next door in Vietnam. Kennedy had to make a decision fast:

"If we have to fight in Southeast Asia, let's fight in Vietnam. The Vietnamese, at least, are committed and will fight."

VIETNAM. When the French left the region, the country was partitioned. The North was controlled by Ho Chi Minh, a Communist who had led the fight for independence. If free elections had been held as scheduled, Ho would probably have taken power in the South as well. Instead, President Eisenhower installed a pro-Western leader, Ngo Dinh Diem, who had previously supported the French. A Roman Catholic, Diem was an odd choice to lead this mostly Buddhist country.

In the North, the Communists soon cracked down on religious and other freedoms. Peasants rose up in revolt and were massacred. Nearly one million people fled to the South, where life was freer—but also more corrupt.

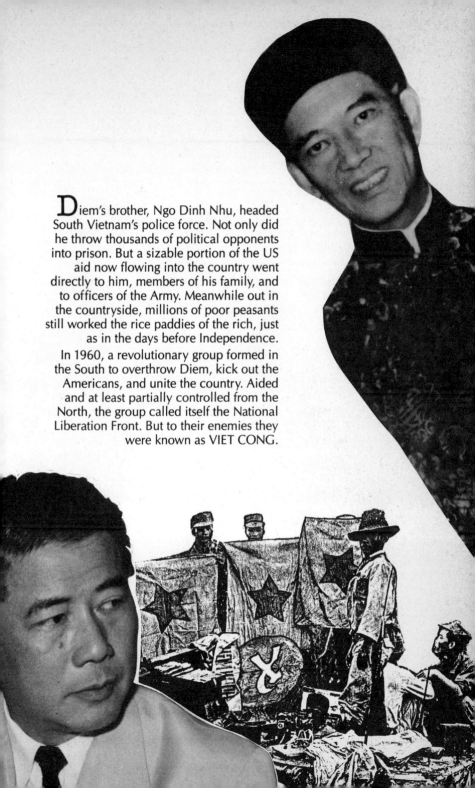

Diem's brother, Ngo Dinh Nhu, headed South Vietnam's police force. Not only did he throw thousands of political opponents into prison. But a sizable portion of the US aid now flowing into the country went directly to him, members of his family, and to officers of the Army. Meanwhile out in the countryside, millions of poor peasants still worked the rice paddies of the rich, just as in the days before Independence.

In 1960, a revolutionary group formed in the South to overthrow Diem, kick out the Americans, and unite the country. Aided and at least partially controlled from the North, the group called itself the National Liberation Front. But to their enemies they were known as VIET CONG.

JFK had carefully read the revolutionary writings of Mao and Castro's *compadre* Che Guevara. He realized that simply killing guerrillas will not win an unconventional "twilight" war. The government must offer its people something worth fighting for. To really succeed, the national army had to win the *hearts and minds* of its people. Traditionalists in the US military tended to see things differently:

Grab 'em good by the short and curlies, and their hearts and minds will follow.

Nevertheless, Kennedy pressured the Vietnamese to make essential reforms. He had little success. On the military front, he authorized the formation of Special Forces units, known as Green Berets, that were trained in counter-insurgency warfare. They were taught to speak the language of the country, live off the land, and operate behind enemy lines. Kennedy eventually sent hundreds of Green Berets and 15,000 other military advisors to the 'Nam.

Yet JFK knew military support was not enough to turn the tide in the Third World. He got the US Congress to broadly increase foreign aid around the globe. And he held consultations with dozens of national leaders from the new nations of Asia and Africa—many of whom remembered Kennedy's opposition to colonialism. Even longtime opponents of US policy were now forced to look at America in a more positive light.

The new President also pushed for the creation of the Peace Corps, which was an immediate success. Thousands of young American volunteers were sent overseas to help people better their own lives. The Peace Corps' usual mission was to help improve literacy, health care, farming, home construction and roads. But volunteers often learned as much as they taught. And their youthful idealism help improve the image of the US around the world.

In Latin America, Kennedy initiated the Alliance for Progress, which was intended to eliminate some of the misery that breeds violent revolution. The purpose of the Alliance was to encourage Latin nations to institute long-overdue social reforms such as democratization and land reform. If fear of Castro was the stick that drove change—JFK hoped that a half billion dollars in American aid would be the carrot. In Mexico City, the President told a huge cheering crowd that:

> "New factories and machinery mean little to
> the family without a home, to the student
> without a meal, to a farmer who even gives up
> hope of finally owning the land he tills."

This message won millions of friends for the United States throughout the hemisphere. In fact, John F. Kennedy was probably the second most popular leader in Latin America. The first, especially to the young, was still none other than his old enemy, Fidel Castro.

Cuba refused to simply fade away. For the Kennedys, Castro had become a personal issue. When the Bay of Pigs went sour, for example, Bobby angrily told his brother, "They can't do this to you." The question was who would be the leaders of change in the world: the brothers Kennedy or the brothers Castro, Fidel and Raúl?

Operation MONGOOSE was the name of the secret US plan to bring down the Castro regime. Bobby Kennedy was placed in charge. Hundreds of Americans, thousands of Cuban emigres, a small navy and air force, and nearly $100 million a year were assigned to the task. It eventually became the largest CIA operation in the world. Working with agents on the island, MONGOOSE was responsible for burning tons of sugar cane and other acts of sabotage. Incidents were provoked to increase tensions between Cubans and Soviet personnel.

Bizarre acts of terrorism were also contemplated—from the drugging of farm workers to using chemicals on Castro that would make his beard fall out. This was supposed to damage the Cuban leader's machismo and lead to his downfall. Even assassination was considered, though the President eventually ruled that out.

In truth, MONGOOSE backfired completely. Instead of weakening Castro's position, the Cuban leader used the operation as an excuse to get more Soviet support. By early October 1962, there were 20,000 Russian troops on the island, supported by 150 jets, 350 tanks, and over a thousand heavy guns and anti-aircraft. But American surveillance revealed something even more ominous being unloaded in Havana harbor:

Missiles. In early October, aerial photographs over Cuba confirmed the existence of Soviet ballistic missiles capable of hitting targets up to 2,000 miles away.

The nuclear warheads for these missiles, however, did not yet seem to be in place. This last bit of information gave President Kennedy the luxury of time—time to deliberate on a course of action, time to put plans into motion, time to avert the Crisis before the first shot was fired.

JFK had learned a lot since the Bay of Pigs. Now he made sure that he would hear *all* the options before he acted. Key people were summoned from the Departments of State and Defense, the Armed Forces, the varied intelligence agencies, and his Cabinet. The group was dubbed the Executive Committee of the National Security Council—ExCom for short. Over the next two weeks of the Crisis they camped out at the State Department, tirelessly arguing over policy.

The Hawks, aggressive hardliners led by the military, advised immediate action against Cuba: a *surgical* airstrike on the missiles or a full-scale American invasion. The Soviet threat would be eliminated at one stroke, they insisted. Then the two super-powers could talk it over.

Bobby took the position of the more conciliatory Doves. He insisted that a sneak attack would confuse the whole question of US self-defense. It would make America look to the world like an aggressor, like the Japanese at Pearl Harbor. There had to be some other way.

JFK was tense, humorless. There was none of his usual coolness under pressure. More than any of his advisors, the President clearly saw the Crisis in political and diplomatic terms. Not as a simple military problem.

2 MISSILE TRANSPORTERS

6 MISSILE TRANSPORTERS

PROB IRBM PROPELLANT TRAILERS

ERECTOR

3 MISSILE TRANSPORTERS

The missiles, when installed, would add little to the Soviet arsenal. But politically their weight would be felt in every decision made by the US government. The weapons were a *psychological* dagger at America's heart. What if the Cubans got their hands on the missiles? And what if Khrushchev got away with this—only 90 miles away from our shores—where would America draw the line?

This time the President did not cave into the Hawks. He continued to ask the hard questions, such as: What would happen if Soviet personnel were killed in the attack? Would Khrushchev have any option then except to retaliate? Was there a way to get rid of the missiles that left the Soviet leader an "escape hatch," a way to withdraw gracefully?

After days of deliberation, Kennedy chose a plan of action. A naval blockade would be placed around Cuba. Ships heading for Cuba would be stopped and inspected. Those carrying weapons would be turned around.

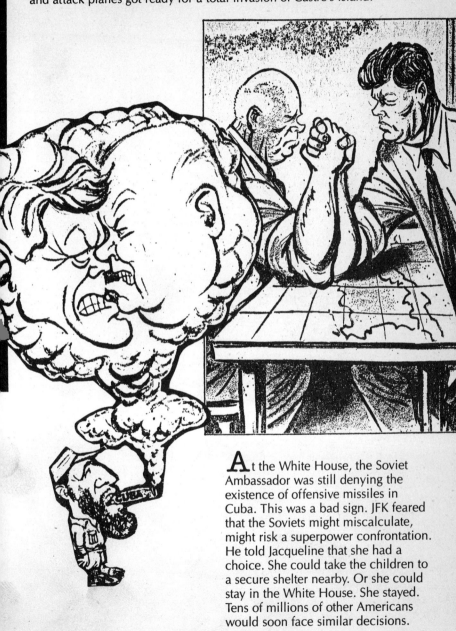

Kennedy knew that Khrushchev would have to react. But the reaction would not necessarily be military. Still, US Armed Forces around the world were placed on total alert. And in case the blockade failed—troops, ships, and attack planes got ready for a total invasion of Castro's island.

At the White House, the Soviet Ambassador was still denying the existence of offensive missiles in Cuba. This was a bad sign. JFK feared that the Soviets might miscalculate, might risk a superpower confrontation. He told Jacqueline that she had a choice. She could take the children to a secure shelter nearby. Or she could stay in the White House. She stayed. Tens of millions of other Americans would soon face similar decisions.

○ monday ○

On Monday evening at 7:00 P.M., President Kennedy went on national television. He told America about the Soviet missiles, and called them a "deliberately provocative and unjustifiable change in the status quo which cannot be accepted by this country, if our courage and commitments are ever to be trusted again by either friend or foe."

Publicly, he asked Premier Khrushchev to eliminate this clandestine, reckless, and provocative threat to world peace. And he closed his speech by declaring:

"Our goal is not the victory of might, but the vindication of right."

○ tuesday ○

On Tuesday morning the world was still there. Communications continued between the White House and the Kremlin. But 14 Russian ships were rapidly approaching the line of quarantine—500 miles outside of Cuba. The President, his brother, and the rest of ExCom waited breathlessly.

At precisely 10:25 A.M., word came that the Soviet ships had stopped dead in the water.

Through diplomatic channels, Kennedy assured Khrushchev that if the Soviets cooperated with the blockade, the US would avoid any direct confrontation. On Wednesday, however, there was a confrontation of a different kind at the United Nations. US Ambassador Adlai Stevenson demanded that the Soviets admit that they had placed offensive missiles in Cuba. When they refused, Stevenson revealed the aerial photos and pointed out:

"You are in the courtroom of world opinion right now."

friday

On Friday, the Soviets sent an informal message to President Kennedy with an offer: If the Soviets removed their missiles, would the US agree not to invade Cuba? Kennedy continued to deliberate. Later that day, Khrushchev officially made the same proposal. If the US called off its fleet, he promised, everything would change immediately. Then comparing world tension to a noose, the Premier added:

"Let us not only relax the forces pulling on the ends of the rope, let us take measures to untie that knot. We are ready for this."

On Saturday, however, a jarring new message came from Khrushchev. This one was far from conciliatory. It demanded that the US pull its missile force out of Turkey in return for a Soviet pullout from Cuba. Meanwhile, the FBI reported that personnel at the Soviet Embassy in New York were frantically destroying sensitive documents. Were they getting ready for war?

In reality, JFK had ordered the obsolete US missiles in Turkey withdrawn months before. Their military value was minimal. Yet the threatening tone of Khrushchev's second message was unacceptable.

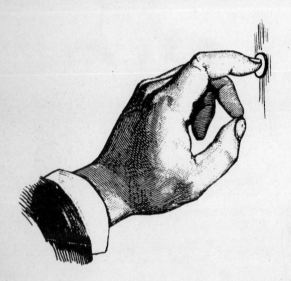

Kennedy was practically ready to order an attack on the missiles in Cuba. But at the very last minute he held back. As Chief Executive, he understood Khrushchev's problem better than anyone else in ExCom. The Soviet leader's own Hawks were probably putting pressure on him, the President realized.

It was Bobby who then suggested that JFK simply ignore Khrushchev's second message. Jack agreed. He sent a message to the Soviets that guaranteed Cuban security—if the missiles were withdrawn. There was no word about the American weapons in Turkey. But the message stressed American desires for "reducing tensions and halting the arms race."

Informally, Bobby admitted to the Soviet Ambassador that the President had wanted to remove missiles from Turkey months before. When the Crisis was over, he said, it was likely that those missiles would also be removed. Which is exactly what happened.

Again Khrushchev wired Kennedy. Now his response was positive. He agreed to pull out the missiles from Cuba. Two days later, JFK formally ordered the termination of Operation MONGOOSE. The deal was working.

Fidel Castro complained that the Soviets acted without consulting him. But the rest of the world breathed a little easier.

The following year, the US and the USSR signed a treaty that banned the testing of nuclear weapons in the open air. It was the first formal agreement of its kind between the two superpowers, and a major arms control breakthrough. Another agreement created a telecommunications "Hotline" between Washington and Moscow, so that the American and Soviet leadership could talk directly in a serious Crisis.

"Let us never negotiate out of fear," JFK had declared at his Inauguration. "But never let us fear to negotiate." This promise he had kept in full.

МИРНОЕ СОСУЩЕСТВОВАНИЕ

The peaceful settlement of the Cuban Missile Crisis marked the end of the Cold War between the US and the USSR. A new phase in superpower relations was just beginning that some called Peaceful Coexistence. The differences between the superpowers did not suddenly disappear—nor would they in the future. But never again would the US and the Soviets be eyeball to eyeball in a life and death struggle. Each now had to respect the other's right to exist:

> "For in the final analysis, our most basic
> link is that we all inhabit this small
> planet. We all breathe the same air. We
> all cherish our children's future. And
> we are all mortal."

Chapter 4: **The Struggle at Home**

The Civil Rights Movement has its own history and destiny, martyrs and prophets. John F. Kennedy did not create the Movement; nor could he have stopped it, even if he had wanted to. Yet his active support came at a crucial time in the struggle for equality. And it encouraged a generation of black people to push even harder against the barriers of injustice—until, like the walls of Jericho, they came tumbling down.

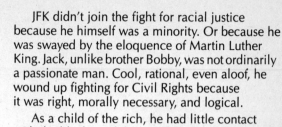

JFK didn't join the fight for racial justice because he himself was a minority. Or because he was swayed by the eloquence of Martin Luther King. Jack, unlike brother Bobby, was not ordinarily a passionate man. Cool, rational, even aloof, he wound up fighting for Civil Rights because it was right, morally necessary, and logical.

As a child of the rich, he had little contact with the blacks and their problems. In the Congress he had voted for every Civil Rights law that came along, almost as a matter of course. To his mind, discrimination against a person on the basis of color simply made no sense. When he did think about black people it was usually in terms of the black vote—the same way he thought about every other ethnic group.

119

As candidate for President, he had wanted to treat Civil Rights as just another issue. Plenty of Americans were disadvantaged. And he wanted to help them all.

For the poor, he wanted a higher minimum wage, job training, and other assistance programs.

For the hungry of Appalachia and elsewhere, he demanded adequate nutrition—a campaign promise he'd made down in West Virginia.

For the homeless he pushed legislation for low cost federally funded housing.

For the elderly he worked to increase social security and to establish Medicare.

And for women, he called for an end to job discrimination on the basis of sex.

Black people, of course, had to face all of those problems—plus the extra burden of racial injustice. JFK first became truly aware of this fact while preparing for the Nixon TV debate. It was then that he learned these chilling statistics:

"The Negro baby born in America today…has about one-half as much chance of completing high school as a white baby born in the same place on the same day, one-third as much chance of completing college…twice as much chance of becoming unemployed…a life expectancy which is seven years shorter, and the prospects of earning only half as much."

CIVIL LIBERTIES

IN THE UNITED STATES

That blacks were so short-changed by the American Dream shocked and angered him. This pattern of discrimination was worse than abominable. It was also *illogical*. Just when he wanted to get the country moving again, here was a criminal waste of so much talent and energy. In a television speech he declared, "We do not want a Negro who could be a doctor, in a city short of doctors, working as a messenger." Racial injustice was a blot on the entire nation.

At his Inauguration the following year, JFK was angered that there wasn't a single black face in the Coast Guard unit marching past the reviewing stand. The new President ordered an investigation of racism in every branch of government. And he authorized the immediate desegregation of the Guard, as well as a special effort to attract black recruits.

Kennedy insisted on similar affirmative action in all government departments and agencies: Treasury, Foreign Service, Labor, State, and others. Not only did he increase the number of black lawyers in the Justice Department by 700%. But he was the first President to appoint black Ambassadors to European— as well as African—nations.

In the first months of his Administration, JFK also dealt decisively with other areas of job discrimination. The new Administration ordered all companies doing business with the Federal Government to immediately end racism in hiring. And with the stroke of a pen, Kennedy helped integrate over 20 million jobs.

Under ordinary circumstances, these acts would've been hailed by the Civil Rights Movement as daring, noble, even heroic—instead of merely a good beginning. But the times, the turbulent 1960s, were anything but ordinary.

Fortunately, John F. Kennedy was no ordinary leader either. He could grow, change. Gradually, as the Civil Rights Movement began its long march to freedom, JFK found himself moving from the sidelines—to the frontlines. And as he did, the man and his Presidency took on a moral dimension that is still honored a quarter century after his death.

The roots of the Movement itself went back to the days before the Civil War, to leaders such as Frederick Douglass. A runaway slave, Douglass became a leading spokesman for the abolition of slavery. In his weekly newspaper, *The North Star*, Douglass was one of the first to denounce racism as destructive to the humanity of both blacks and whites.

Lincoln's Emancipation Proclamation raised the hopes of millions of Southern blacks. But the outcome of the Civil War left them disillusioned. No longer slaves, many found themselves working the same plantations—now as tenant farmers. Living conditions were often worse since they were no longer valuable "property," and could easily be replaced.

In towns and cities, restrictive "Jim Crow" laws kept blacks as second class citizens. This meant separate housing, schools, churches, transportation, and employment. Peaceful redress of grievances was blocked by the fact that fewer than 10% of Southern blacks were allowed to vote.

124

And when the law failed, there was always the terror of the Ku Klux Klan.

In the early 1900s, W.E.B. Dubois helped form the National Association for the Advancement of Colored People. Dubois, an intellectual and a committed socialist, hoped that the NAACP could use the power of the law to eradicate discrimination.

In the 1920s, Marcus Garvey spoke out for black economic independence. He encouraged minorities to start their own businesses—which eventually even included a shipping company, The Black Star Line.

In 1954, the US Supreme Court ruled that segregated schools were illegal. The Court declared that the racist concept of "separate but equal" was a lie. In fact, segregated facilities for blacks were almost always unequal. Yet throughout the nation—not just in the South—Jim Crow remained the rule.

T hen, December 2, 1955, the courage of one black woman began to rock the foundations of injustice. Rosa Parks was a former secretary of the Montgomery, Alabama, NAACP. One day after work, she simply refused to give up a seat to a white man and move to the crowded back of the bus— reserved for ''coloreds.'' She was immediately arrested.

The black community decided it was time to end the indignity of segregation. A boycott of the buses was declared. Carpools were organized. And people walked. The boycott lasted for thirteen long months, but black people refused to give in. One elderly woman explained:

"I'm not walking for myself. I'm walking for my children and my grandchildren."

An eloquent black minister rose to lead the boycott. His name was Dr. Martin Luther King. His tactic was nonviolence. His purpose was clear:

"...Not to coerce but to correct, not to break bodies or wills but to move hearts."

The success of the boycott spread throughout the South. In 1960, black college students held SIT-INs to integrate public restaurants and other facilities. They were joined by a few brave whites. All had to face arrest and imprisonment, as well as the violence of mobs.

Soon after Kennedy's Inauguration, two integrated busloads of young Civil Rights activists headed South to desegregate interstate transportation. They called themselves Freedom Riders. Once in Alabama, though, both buses were attacked and set on fire. As the young people escaped the smoke, they were badly beaten and bloodied.

All this was happening as JFK was about to meet Khrushchev at the summit in Vienna. Robert Kennedy was in sympathy with the Riders, but he was afraid that any more violence would embarrass the President. So he asked for a temporary halt to the Freedom Rides—a "cooling off" period. James Farmer, an important Civil Rights leader, complained:

"We've been cooling off for 100 years. If we got any cooler we'd be in the deep freeze."

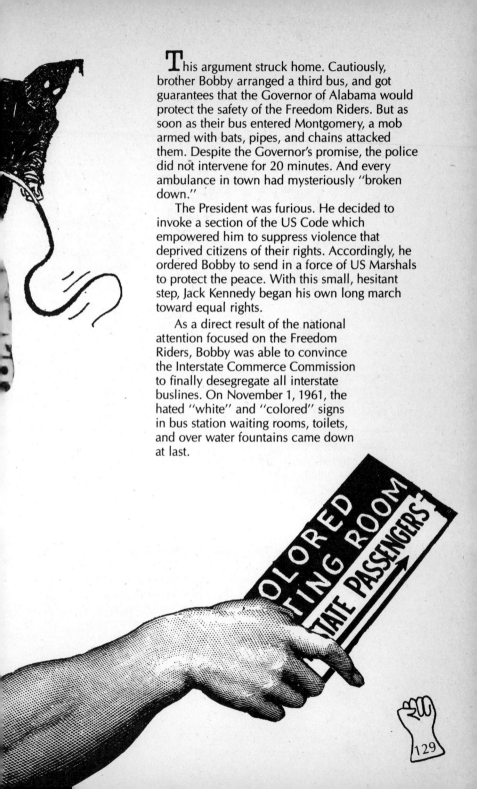

This argument struck home. Cautiously, brother Bobby arranged a third bus, and got guarantees that the Governor of Alabama would protect the safety of the Freedom Riders. But as soon as their bus entered Montgomery, a mob armed with bats, pipes, and chains attacked them. Despite the Governor's promise, the police did not intervene for 20 minutes. And every ambulance in town had mysteriously "broken down."

The President was furious. He decided to invoke a section of the US Code which empowered him to suppress violence that deprived citizens of their rights. Accordingly, he ordered Bobby to send in a force of US Marshals to protect the peace. With this small, hesitant step, Jack Kennedy began his own long march toward equal rights.

As a direct result of the national attention focused on the Freedom Riders, Bobby was able to convince the Interstate Commerce Commission to finally desegregate all interstate buslines. On November 1, 1961, the hated "white" and "colored" signs in bus station waiting rooms, toilets, and over water fountains came down at last.

Now the struggle shifted to neighboring Mississippi. The US Supreme Court had ruled that James Meredith, a black man, had to be admitted to the publicly funded—but segregated—State University in Oxford. Governor Ross Barnett desperately tried to save face. He suggested that Meredith be smuggled in at night. Or that US Marshals actually hold a gun to his own head and that photos be taken to prove that fact.

Weeks of negotiations went nowhere. President Kennedy wanted to avoid a confrontation between the State and the Federal government. But when talks broke down, he ordered 550 Marshals into Oxford to enforce the law.

The Governor had assured him that National Guard troops would *not* be needed. But when Meredith tried to register at "Ole Miss," the college was overrun by thousands of white hoodlums. The 200 State policemen Barnett promised suddenly disappeared from the scene.

A pitched battle broke out in which more than a hundred US Marshals were injured, 35 with gunshot wounds. A newsman and a townsman were killed. After hours of delay, National Guard troops finally arrived to put down the riot. The following morning, Meredith passed through a jeering crowd to be registered.

JFK was angered that the Governor and his mob had ignored the Supreme Court, taking the law into their own hands. But Robert Kennedy had a more intense, gut reaction. In anger, he wondered about the Soviet missiles that had just been discovered in Cuba. Hopefully, he asked:

"Can they reach Oxford, Mississippi?"

The more the Kennedys learned about the way blacks were being treated in the South, the more committed they became to the Civil Rights cause. But it would take more than a few skirmishes to get rid of segregation.

The next showdown took place in nearby Alabama. Martin Luther King had called industrial Birmingham the most racist big city in the US:

"Birmingham is so segregated, we're within a cab ride of being in Johannesburg, South Africa."

He believed that if racism could be undermined here, the walls of prejudice would fall all over the South. Dr. King and the leaders of the other Civil Rights groups began planning months in advance. Nonviolent resistance would be the weapon they would use, the same force that Gandhi used to free his people from British rule.

"Through our pain, we will make them see their injustice."

—Gandhi

Once and for all, the Movement would show the world that black people will no longer tolerate discrimination. Hundreds were required to swear that, regardless of the provocation, they would come and go in peace. And if necessary, they would fill the jails of Birmingham. Dr. King explained why this strategy would eventually overcome:

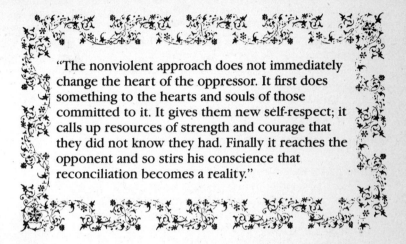

"The nonviolent approach does not immediately change the heart of the oppressor. It first does something to the hearts and souls of those committed to it. It gives them new self-respect; it calls up resources of strength and courage that they did not know they had. Finally it reaches the opponent and so stirs his conscience that reconciliation becomes a reality."

The Movement was prepared to use every possible tactic: parades, petitions, boycotts, and sit-ins. Dr. King expected that the struggle would be a hard one—but he didn't realize how hard. For opposing him was the vicious Birmingham Chief of Police, Theophilus Eugene "Bull" Connor:

"Damn the law! Down here I'm the law."

133

For the first month, Bull Connor decided to combat nonviolence with nonviolence. Each day the police peacefully arrested the marchers and escorted them to the waiting paddy wagons. Brutality was kept to a minimum. But Connor could control himself and his police force for only so long.

After a solid month of nonviolent demonstrations and thousands of arrests, the walls of injustice still were standing. Civil Rights leaders now criticized Kennedy for doing nothing to help the cause in Birmingham. JFK met with a group of black activists led by writer James Baldwin, who angrily accused the President of pulling back from his commitment to equality. Was Jack really a friend? Or was he more concerned with his reelection campaign? Others were asking the same questions.

JFK tried to explain that there was nothing he could do. No mobs threatened to riot, no laws had been broken yet by the police, no court orders defied. Anxiously, he watched the events in Birmingham—waiting for the right moment to intervene. It soon came.

On May 2, 1963, more than a thousand young demonstrators were arrested downtown, literally filling the jails. Next day, another thousand began marching and chanting Freedom songs—when they were ordered to stop. They refused. Bull Connor ordered fire hoses turned on the men, women, and children, knocking them all to the sidewalk.

A crowd of black spectators across the street protested, shouting threats and throwing stones and bottles at the police. Bull Connor now completely lost control. Enraged, he set police dogs on the defenseless marchers, grinning while the cops continued to club prostrate men and women to the ground. Even children weren't spared.

Pictures from the scene shocked the world. Like most of the nation, President Kennedy was sickened by what he saw. But he also realized that things in Birmingham had changed overnight. Now America would support practically any action he would take to stop the brutality. And to Martin Luther King he said, with more than a trace of irony:

"The civil rights movement owes Bull Connor as much as it owes Abraham Lincoln."

JFK sent representatives to Birmingham to drive a bargain: The demonstrations would end if the white power structure would just make some move that recognized the existence of blacks—and acknowledged their humanity. On May 10, Birmingham finally agreed to desegregate lunch rooms, rest rooms, store fitting rooms, and drinking fountains. It was a beginning.

But the next night the terror began. A bomb destroyed the home of Dr. King's brother. Another ripped apart Movement headquarters. Then riots broke out all over the city. The police focused its attack on the black neighborhoods. Immediately, JFK ordered troops into the city to keep the peace—and to enforce the agreement, which he declared "recognized the fundamental right of all citizens to be accorded equal treatment and opportunity."

George Wallace, Alabama's racist Governor, wasn't about to just surrender. On June 11, Wallace threatened to stand in the doorway of the State University in order to block court-ordered desegregation. It was a hollow gesture. This time President Kennedy was ready.

Hundreds of US Marshals surrounded the University. Thousands of US troops waited in helicopters nearby in case riots broke out. After his big moment in front of the cameras, Wallace had to step aside. Integration went on as planned. And that very evening, JFK went on television with a challenge to the whole nation:

"We are confronted primarily with a moral issue. It is as old as the Scriptures and it is clear as the American Constitution. The heart of the question is whether all Americans are to be afforded equal rights and equal opportunities: whether we are going to treat our fellow Americans as we want to be treated."

The President backed up this statement with an announcement long awaited by black people: "I shall ask the Congress of the United States to act," he declared, "to make a commitment it has not fully made in this century to the proposition that race has no place in American life or law."

JFK knew that his new Civil Rights Act was going to face an uphill fight. The Act would outlaw discrimination in education, employment, housing, public accommodation, and voting. Kennedy hoped that many Republican Congressmen would support the sweeping new law. Otherwise, the South would defeat in Washington what it could not beat down in Dixie.

Despite what many cynics believe, the President had already suffered politically for his support of Civil Rights. Polls showed that 36 percent of the voters felt he was moving too fast on the race issue, while only 18 percent felt he was moving too slow. And his popularity reflected this. From his near 80 percent approval rating around the time of the Bay of Pigs, Kennedy was now down to only 53 percent.

"This issue could cost me the election, but we're not turning back."

The March on Washington, planned for August 28, was the biggest Civil Rights rally in history. After initial fears that the March might hurt his new law's chance of passage, Kennedy announced his full support. The government of the United States and the city of Washington opened their arms to the demonstrators and made them welcome.

A quarter million people—black and white, rich and poor, Christian and Jew, from every region of the country—gathered peacefully on that day. "We Shall Overcome" was the theme song of the March. And the most memorable words were spoken by the black minister whose actions and beliefs symbolized the courage and dignity of his whole people:

"I have a dream that...little black boys and girls will be able to join hands with little white boys and girls as sisters and brothers. I have a dream today..."

Martin Luther King called on all Americans to let freedom ring throughout the land. And he closed with the hope that one day all of God's children will join together "and sing in the words of the old Negro spiritual, 'Free at last! Free at last, thank God Almighty, we're free at last.'"

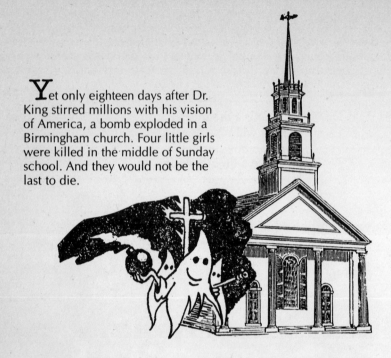

Yet only eighteen days after Dr. King stirred millions with his vision of America, a bomb exploded in a Birmingham church. Four little girls were killed in the middle of Sunday school. And they would not be the last to die.

JFK tried to push the Civil Rights Act through Congress. His legislative record had always been poor. He had no talent for the give and take of Congressional politics. And the leaders of the Senate and the House were considerably older and more conservative than the President. To make things worse, many were Southerners—who threatened to kill the new law in committee or fillibuster it to death before it ever came to a vote.

Nevertheless, Kennedy was happy to see that the Act had finally squeaked out of a deadlocked Congressional subcommittee. It arrived at the powerful House Rules Committee on November 21, 1963—the same day the President left for a speechmaking tour of Texas.

The Democratic Party in the Lone Star State—like the rest of the South—was practically in revolt. Though the President was praised for his strength in the Cuban Missile Crisis, millions of Texans felt that JFK was moving far too fast on Civil Rights. Many threatened to abandon the party completely and support the Republicans. Even Vice President Johnson couldn't keep the different factions in line anymore.

Kennedy recalled the close election of 1960. He feared that losing Texas in the '64 election might also mean losing the White House. So despite warnings of mass protests against him, JFK ventured South.

This time he traveled with the First Lady, who previously tried to avoid these political trips. Jackie felt uneasy in the White House, alienated, as though she lived in a fishbowl with all the fish outside. Increasingly, the relationship between her and the President grew cooler.

Tragedy brought them closer together. In August, 1963, the Kennedy's third child, Patrick, was born prematurely and died after only two days. Jack was distraught. He wept openly, seized hold of the little casket, and had to be escorted away from the grave site.

He had always lavished affection on little Caroline and John Junior. Now his appreciation was extended to Jackie as well. And he was delighted when she agreed to accompany him to Dallas. But the First Lady was worried.

Jackie had seen the local newspaper with a full page tirade against JFK—surrounded by an ominous black border. The ad was paid for by angry Right Wingers who accused the President of being in league with the Communists. It didn't directly mention Civil Rights, but it attacked both Kennedys for persecuting loyal Americans.

The President tried to shrug it all off:

> "We're heading into nut country today. But Jackie, if somebody wants to shoot from a window with a rifle, nobody can stop it, so why worry about it?"

Tens of thousands lined the motorcade route, holding signs of welcome and cheering. Then, as the President's limousine rolled in front of the School Book Depository building—there was the sound of gunfire.

John Fitzgerald Kennedy, age 46, President of the United States for little more than a thousand days, was dead.

Only a week after JFK's assassination, the new President, Lyndon B. Johnson told the nation:

"No memorial oration or eulogy could more eloquently honor President Kennedy's memory than the earliest possible passage of the civil rights bill for which he fought so long."

A spirit of national reconciliation seemed to sweep through the country, softening the hearts of Northerners and Southerners, Democrats and Republicans alike. Less than a year after the death of John F. Kennedy, on July 2, 1964, the legislation that Martin Luther King called THE SECOND EMANCIPATION PROCLAMATION was finally signed into law.

Chapter 5: The Legacy

"...The greatest enemy of the truth is very often not the lie—deliberate, contrived, and dishonest—but the myth, persistent, persuasive, and unrealistic."

—JFK

One out of three Americans alive today was not born when President Kennedy spoke those words, back in May of 1962. What should young people, as well as the rest of us, know about JFK and his legacy?

The truth is a good place to start. Jack Kennedy wanted the whole truth to be known, so that we could learn from his mistakes, as well as his successes. That's why he gave these very specific instructions to Ted Sorenson, his friend and biographer.

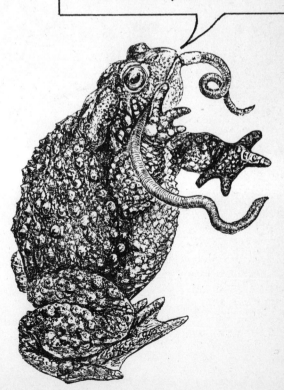

"You are obliged to tell our story in a truthful way...with all our blemishes and warts, all those things that may not be so immediately attractive."

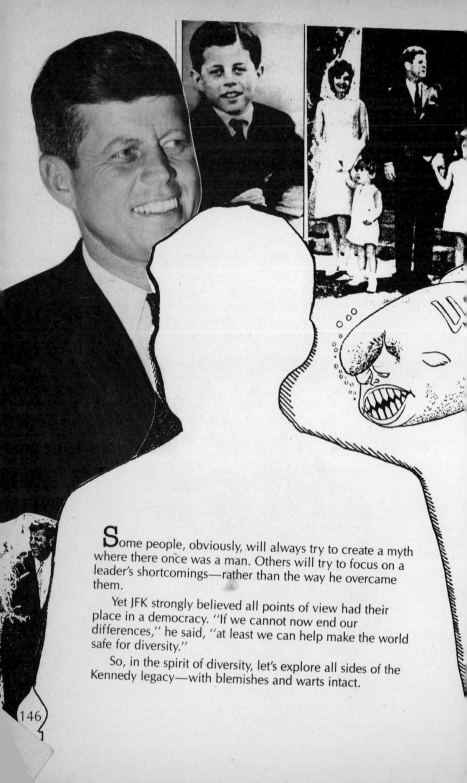

Some people, obviously, will always try to create a myth where there once was a man. Others will try to focus on a leader's shortcomings—rather than the way he overcame them.

Yet JFK strongly believed all points of view had their place in a democracy. "If we cannot now end our differences," he said, "at least we can help make the world safe for diversity."

So, in the spirit of diversity, let's explore all sides of the Kennedy legacy—with blemishes and warts intact.

JFK Bought The Election!

Kennedy himself alluded to this charge. During the campaign he jokingly claimed to have received a telegram from his "generous daddy" which warned: "Don't buy a single vote more than necessary. I'll be damned if I'm going to pay for a landslide."

Money, as PJ Kennedy discovered a century ago, is the fuel of politics. During JFK's primary battles, the family fortune was definitely a great asset. It bought him an airplane, and helped pay for ads, staff, and supplies. Yet Kennedy money did *not* buy the Presidency. Richard Nixon spent an equivalent amount of cash—and lost anyway.

147

Kennedy Was A Wire Tapper!

As a Congressman, JFK actually introduced a bill that would have outlawed all wiretaps. Yet as President, he freely authorized electronic surveillance for a variety of "national security" reasons. These included bugging suspected Soviet agents and subversives, as well as organized crime figures such as Jimmy Hoffa—who was actually taped discussing the best ways to kill his arch-enemy, Attorney General Robert Kennedy.

JFK clearly trusted himself to use wiretaps in a way consistent with the Constitution. But perhaps he didn't realize that the same "national security" arguments could easily be abused by the Presidents who followed him, notably his old rival Richard Nixon.

JFK Managed The Press!

He certainly tried to, anyway. Kennedy realized the importance of the media for creating national support. And as a former newsman himself, Jack usually had great rapport with reporters. As President, he skillfully used his personal ties—as well as promise of greater access to White House exclusives—to reward friends of the New Frontier, and to punish its foes.

Yet JFK made himself available to the press more than any President in recent history. And he eventually also came to know the risks of trying to manage a free press. During the Bay of Pigs Crisis, the President was angered by news leaks mentioning the invasion. Later he admitted, "I should have realized that there was no way of keeping a clandestine operation like this secret in a free democracy. And that's the way it should be."

149

Kennedy's Space Program: Propaganda Not Pioneering

Just two months after his Inauguration, JFK watched the Soviets send the first man into space, cosmonaut Yuri Gargarin. This triumph gave Russia a great propaganda boost around the world. In desperation, Kennedy asked his science advisors, "Is there any space program which promises dramatic results which we can win?"

Assured that America's technology was up to the task, the President committed the nation to landing a man on the moon by the end of the decade. Kennedy was genuinely interested in scientific developments and their applications. And he also felt that if Space were part of the New Frontier. America's astronauts would be its pioneers—whose exploits would inspire all humanity. The irony, of course, was that the President who actually reaped the propaganda benefit of the Lunar Landing in 1969 was Richard Nixon.

The Alliance For Progress: Too Little, Too Late

As a means of improving the US image in Latin America, the Alliance succeeded brilliantly. But as a practical tool to bring democracy, social reform, and modernization to the hemisphere—it failed miserably. But was Kennedy truly responsible?

Too often, the US officials who administered the Alliance were the same people who had previously supported the status quo. And even the President couldn't change US bureaucracy overnight. To make matters worse, Latin American leaders frequently would channel Alliance funds into pet projects, and sometimes even into their own pockets. Some dictators actually refused aid if it meant sharing the land or loosening their grip over the country.

Perhaps the US would have been better off committing itself to a program of gradual—rather than immediate—change in Latin America. Maybe failure of the Alliance was just another example of Kennedy's impatience with the slow spread of democratization through the world.

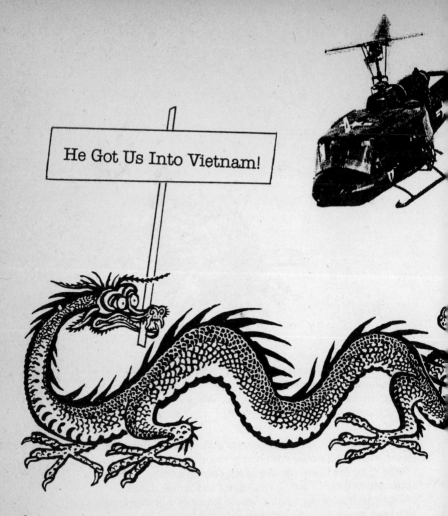

He Got Us Into Vietnam!

Actually, Eisenhower got us into Vietnam. But it was John F. Kennedy who put us *deeper* into that quagmire.

Indochina exercised a powerful fascination over him since his trip there as a Senator. Even then he was calling for the creation of a democratic alternative to colonialism and Communism. A decade later, as President, he was still wishing for the impossible.

Not only did Vietnam's President Diem refuse necessary reforms. But millions of Vietnamese continued to identify with their northern "cousins," rather than their American protectors.

To make matters worse, the State Department, CIA, and the military had been predicting imminent victory for over a decade. It was hard to get the straight facts about such a complicated situation. Once, when two advisors returned from Saigon with radically different impressions, Kennedy asked, "Are you sure you were on the same plane?"

In 1963, Diem, a Catholic, had the insensitivity to crack
down on Buddhist holiday celebrations. Several monks
burned themselves publicly in protest. JFK, like the rest of the
world, was horrified. But Diem's sister in law joked to the
press about scheduling other "barbecues." Unrest spread
until Diem's generals overthrew his regime—with tacit US
approval!—and then assassinated him.

A few months before his own assassination, Jack Kennedy
was finally able to set up a network of trusted intelligence
sources. They gave the President information the CIA could
or would not provide. The US had already withdrawn 1,000
advisors to protest Diem's refusal to reform. JFK later
promised Congressional leaders that he'd pull out the rest
soon after the 1964 election. No one knows for certain
whether or not he could've kept that pledge.

153

JFK Never Knew His Own Limits

"Let every nation know," Jack Kennedy declared at his Inauguration, "...that we shall pay any price, bear any burden, meet any hardship, support any friend, oppose any foe to assure the survival and success of liberty."

JFK's view of the world was formed in the crucible of World War II. He'd seen the folly and failure of the English leaders who failed to stand up to Hitler. What Kennedy learned was summed up like this, "The only thing necessary for the triumph of evil is for good men to do nothing."

Accordingly, Kennedy believed that America must assist the peoples of the world to resist Communist tyranny—as well as help correct the social scourges that promote it. And he also insisted that America itself must set an example at home of the benefits of freedom.

154

But his enthusiasm for democracy sometimes blinded him. JFK failed to realize that American political institutions were not always exportable, especially to impoverished peoples with different traditions and values. And he ignored the harm Western businesses sometimes do to the fragile Third World economies that they dominate.

In the end, President Kennedy began to comprehend the limits of American power and his own influence: We were not omniscient, omnipotent. We, who were only 6 percent of the world's population, could not hope to impose our will on the rest of humanity. Equally important, JFK learned:

> "...That we cannot right every wrong or reverse each adversity—and that there cannot be an American solution to every world problem."

155

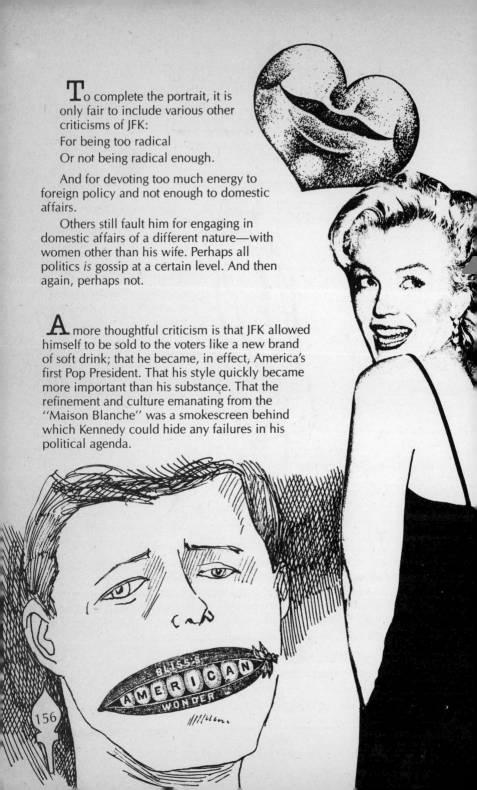

To complete the portrait, it is only fair to include various other criticisms of JFK:

For being too radical

Or not being radical enough.

And for devoting too much energy to foreign policy and not enough to domestic affairs.

Others still fault him for engaging in domestic affairs of a different nature—with women other than his wife. Perhaps all politics *is* gossip at a certain level. And then again, perhaps not.

A more thoughtful criticism is that JFK allowed himself to be sold to the voters like a new brand of soft drink; that he became, in effect, America's first Pop President. That his style quickly became more important than his substance. That the refinement and culture emanating from the "Maison Blanche" was a smokescreen behind which Kennedy could hide any failures in his political agenda.

In the end, however, it is history that will judge him. For decades JFK has eagerly been compared with the Presidents who followed him:

LYNDON JOHNSON—whose Great Society programs did more for America's poor and powerless than Kennedy ever dreamed of. Yet LBJ's stubborn escalation of the Vietnam War left the nation more divided than any time since Lincoln.

RICHARD NIXON—who came to office promising to "bring America together." But his strength and shrewdness were undermined by his stealth. In the end, he *did* unite America—in shame and revulsion over the dirty tricks of Watergate.

GERALD FORD—genial but uncharismatic spokesman for the common man: "I am a Ford, not a Lincoln." Often portrayed as accident prone, his first act in office was to give Nixon a Presidential pardon.

JIMMY CARTER—well intentioned, but poorly prepared for the challenges of an age of "diminished expectations." Architect of the Camp David peace treaty between Israel and Egypt. His political fortunes sank on a tide of inflation, Iranian terror, and Soviet expansionism in Afghanistan.

And finally, **RONALD REAGAN**—America's first "feel good" President since Eisenhower, our previous national grandfather figure. Affable, eloquent, untroubled by facts. Expanded the military, cut social services, and still tried to evoke the aura of the New Frontier. The difference, of course, was that JFK challenged people to ask what they could *do* for America. While Ronald Reagan dared the rich to ask what they could *get* from America.

157

Yet Jack Kennedy's place in history will not be decided by simply measuring his accomplishments against those of the Presidents who followed him.

JFK's greatness flowed directly from his ability to motivate people to believe in themselves, in their institutions, and in their ability to face up to any challenge:

"Democracy is the superior form of government because it is based on a respect for man as a reasonable being."

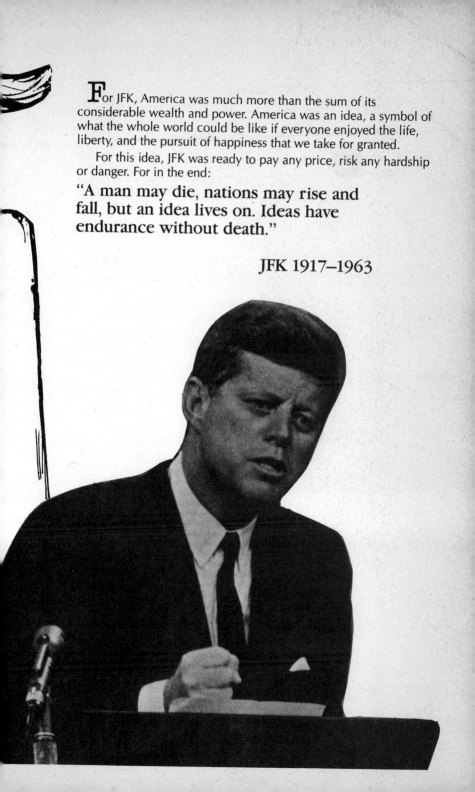

For JFK, America was much more than the sum of its considerable wealth and power. America was an idea, a symbol of what the whole world could be like if everyone enjoyed the life, liberty, and the pursuit of happiness that we take for granted.

For this idea, JFK was ready to pay any price, risk any hardship or danger. For in the end:

"A man may die, nations may rise and fall, but an idea lives on. Ideas have endurance without death."

JFK 1917–1963

Bibliography

Kennedy
>by Theodore C. Sorenson
>>Special Counsel to the Late President
>>Harper & Row, Publishers
>>NY 1965

JFK: The Presidency of John F. Kennedy
>by Herbert S. Parmot
>>The Dial Press
>>NY 1983

John F. Kennedy:
The Promise & The Performance
>by Lewis J. Paper
>>A Da Capo Paperback
>>NY 1987

Johnny, We Hardly Knew Ye:
Memories of John Fitzgerald Kennedy
>by Kenneth P. O'Donnell
>>David F. Powers
>>Little, Brown and Company
>>Boston, Toronto 1972

The Kennedys: An American Drama
>by Peter Collier
>>David Horowitz
>>Warner Books
>>NY 1984

King Remembered
>by Flip Schulke
>>Penelope McPhee
>>Pocket Books
>>NY 1986

Fight for Freedom:
The Story of the NAACP
>by Langston Hughes
>>Berkley Medallion Book
>>NY 1962

Why England Slept
>by John F. Kennedy
>>Dolphin Books/Doubleday
>>Garden City, NY 1962